# The Messenger of Love

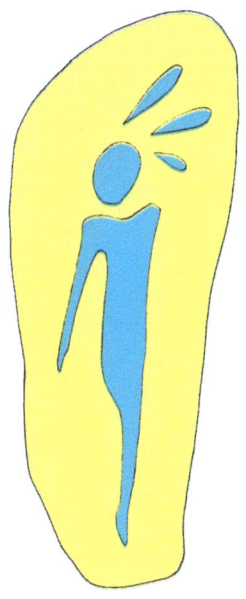

## Stella Longland

a Cave of Clay book

Copyright © Stella Longland 2019

Cover design by Stella Longland ©

second edition 2019
with text revisions

All rights reserved. No part of this publication may be reproduced, stored in a retrieval system, or transmitted in any form or by any means without prior written permission of the copyright owner. Nor can it be circulated in any form of binding or cover other than that in which it is published and without similar condition including this condition being imposed on a subsequent purchaser.

*(first edition 2011 copyright © Stella Longland 2011)*

British Library Cataloguing in Publication Data
A catalogue record for this book is available from the British Library

ISBN 978-1-9999024-1-4

For all my relations
climbing the mountains of light

light tracks
    passing by
        footsteps
            walking
                impressions
                    moving through time
                        leaving traces

*This story was written from the texts of audio tapes
recorded in a state of consciousness
somewhere between
the worlds out there and the world of everyday.*

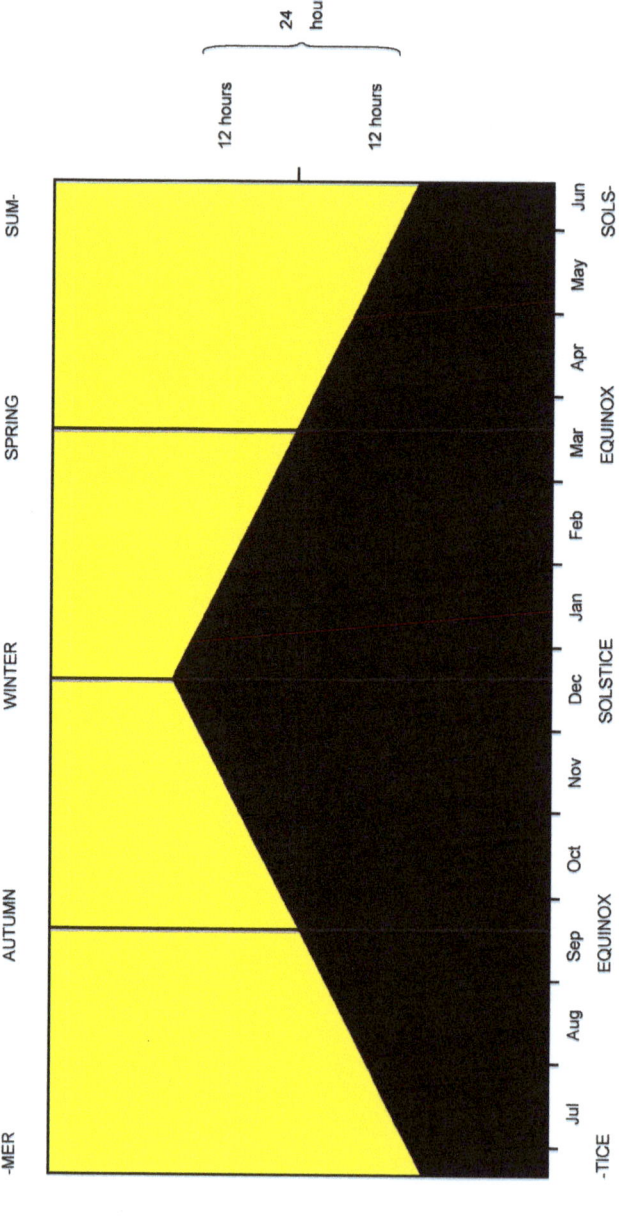

*LIGHT CALENDAR AT 55° LATITUDE in the NORTHERN HEMISPHERE*

*notes on how to use the light calendar:*

*read the light calendar images in the same direction as the text, from left to right.*

*So,*

*a rising line indicates nights getting longer,*
*from midsummer to midwinter.*

                                *This section contains the autumn equinox:*

*a falling line indicates days getting longer,*
*from midwinter to midsummer.*

                                *This section contains the spring equinox:*

*Fascinating things happen to the distribution of the light depending on the latitude, but over the course of a year at any place on the planet the division of the year between the dark and the light is equal.*

*For clarity the light line is represented as straight in these images.*

Contents:

- The Falling Bones
- The Girl
- Interweaving Red and Blue
- The Wake-up Call
- The Name of the Grandfather
- Help is the Colour Yellow
- Gifts from the Southern Hemisphere
- Opening the Gates
- Exploring the Grey
- Knowing the Ropes
- A Modern Jumble
- The Peace Tree
- Dancing the Grandfather

- The Circle of Awareness
- In Relation To
- Tree
- Tree of Smoke
- Looking for Peace
- Crystal Rose
- Returning the White Ribbon
- I Am Killed
- A New Beginning
- The Blue Light
- Between the Sun and the Moon
- Meditative Dreaming
- The Grandfather Dies

*Consult the final 6 pages to find*
  *About Demons*
  *About Intent*
  *About Limits*
  *Other Books by the Author*
  *Index pages*

# The Falling Bones

In the early evening I thought I would lie down and meditate in order to have some contact with my travelling companion, the Coyote. I felt the Coyote arrive and we started to be together. He taught me to focus my attention. He showed me how my mind wanders. I saw that in the meditative travelling it happens spatially and that an actual movement occurs. As the thoughts that diverted me came, my attention would move to the left or the right or up or down or diagonally. He taught me: "Look straight forward steadfastly into the darkness and do not allow yourself to slip."

So, I did this, and I could feel the effect on my mind. It was like looking down a long dark tunnel. I remembered that, in the morning, the image of Joseph Rael, Teacher of Mysteries, had appeared and I had concentrated on that. I began to sense him again and he arrived in my perception in such a way that I felt I was with him, and I felt that I knew him. I was searching through my memory to find where I could have gained this knowledge, as I had only recently heard of him and had never met him, when I noticed the image of an older man with grey hair. I looked at him. He was very different to Joseph. He had a long thin face, a long nose, and long straggly grey hair. A headband was tied round his head with the knot on the right-hand side. He was ancient, and, as if I knew him, I said: "Grandfather!"

I noticed a third person there, a younger man with darker hair. I was struck by the presence of these people. I saw myself in relation to them and it was extremely incongruous because they were so calm, so manly, so full of tradition, and I was just this lightweight girl of european origin. It felt very touching that they should be paying me any attention at all and, addressing the ancient one again, I called softly: "Grandfather."

As I watched he changed. His shoulders lifted as if his body was hung up by them, his clothes became rags and blew in tatters in the wind, his flesh fell away and when his bones were visible, they began to fall and, dropping like leaves, they fell into my body.

## The Girl

This morning I woke from a dream in which I had found myself near the top floor of a very tall building; I was walking into the lift with a small child of about five years old. We walked in and we went down. We came out into a city and we walked along the streets together. She was very shy and wouldn't join in the festivities that were happening there. We walked farther, and, after a while, we came to a place where a group of children were getting ready to dance. My girl, who had grown and was now about ten, wanted to join in that dance and I was very pleased that she seemed less shy.

As she danced, I was able to look at her closely. She was a thin-bodied, dark-skinned girl, with very dark hair. She had a thin face, a lovely angular nose, and dark brown eyes. I noticed that she had put red paint on her face, I thought it was an attempt at make-up and it made me giggle, but no, her forehead and cheeks were covered with bright red shapes made of straight lines. During the dance another girl, who was more experienced, did spiteful tricks like trying to trip her and push her out of the way. The lovely child didn't dance perfectly, but she danced beautifully, with feeling, and the actions of the spiteful child did not affect her at all.

When the dance was over, she came back to me and I congratulated her fervently. For such a small child she was very sensible. She picked up the things that she was carrying with her and she asked: "Oh, where is my ten-inch rule?" This was a silver ruler with inch markers shaped like a triangle that didn't meet in one corner; it was a ruler, but it looked like the musical instrument, a triangle. I said: "Oh, I have put that in my pocket. I'll carry it for you." She still had three things to carry. One was a book, one was a pencil, but I can't remember what the third one was. I said: "Shall I put those in my pockets as well so that you can hold my hand more easily?" But she insisted on carrying all four, and, still managing to hold hands, we were walking down the main street of the city when I said once again: "I was so pleased that you joined in the dance." She said: "Yes, I wasn't very friendly before because the people were strange to me and I didn't understand them, but now we have walked around for a bit and I have got used to them I can join in."

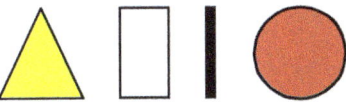

*the four objects*

When the dream ended, I lay thinking about it. I know it is something to do with the Sound Peace Chamber on the Isle of Skye, a building inspired by Joseph's vision of harmony, which I visited recently at the suggestion of my Teacher, Alexander, who is a student of Joseph Rael, Beautiful Painted Arrow. I went there to attend the initiation of the Chamber. It was on the day after I received the falling bones of Ancient Grandfather that I set off to be at that ceremony. They talked there of the spirit of the chambers as a boy, so I don't know who this child is that has come to me now but thinking of her causes many tears and loud crying to burst out of me.

A few days after this dream I attended a weekend seminar held in my local town in the north of England. The seminar was on spiritual healing and was led by my Teacher. On the second day we were to take an altered-state journey to our inner temple. Well, my journey began early in the morning before I left home to drive the fifteen miles to the seminar venue. As I opened the front door of my house and walked in and out, putting things in the car, a woman came past and following her a child leading a white pony. This child had red ribbons tying up her hair in bunches and seeing her brought the dancing girl who had the red paint on her face straight back into my mind. I watched them go by and left shortly after.

In the seminar room later in the day we prepared ourselves. We would travel to our inner sanctuary accompanied by music; the journey began. I was watching the girl with the red ribbons leading the white pony up the street. The pony had a blanket on which was cream-coloured with red and blue threads running through it making a grid pattern. I wondered where I fitted in; I was struggling to find my place in the picture, and, eventually, I was persuaded to see myself as the blue thread in the pattern of the pony's blanket. The pony and the girl had come to collect me and becoming a thread in the blanket was the only way that I was able to travel with them at that time.

We followed a road that ran gently uphill. My companions were innocent and pure, and everything was quiet, clear and divinely simple. We walked up onto a paved platform and went through an entrance between white stone pillars; we had entered a temple and it was blue sky. Amazed at the form that this temple took, I entered the blue, and, able to see more clearly now in the bright light, I looked and looked about me at the endless blue. After a while, a voice said: "Be content with the Blue." I was indeed questing for images, I stopped doing that and I became content with the blue.

After a long, still period of quiet peace, I was taken into darkness, a darkness that contained the colour red. I saw a deep glow of red shining in the black, like coals in a banked-up fire. I examined being in the darkness, and I examined being in the light; both were beautiful, comforting and filled me with awe, but the opportunities in them were not at all similar, and I placed the different feelings that went with each of them into my memory.

Seeing then the colour green, I thought: "Oh, the journey is finished." I had time to ask myself: "How do you know that?" when the music stopped. In answer to my question, I would say that being in the green is being in a world of change and that is my daily life.

In the final session of the seminar, when the sharing crystal came to me, I told this journey and I cried the whole way through. I cried because of the special blessing of simplicity.

### Interweaving Red and Blue

When I went to bed last night there were many immense vertiginous drops into canyons and deep mysterious caves. The Owl was me and I flew with the Owl down into those places. This morning, as I meditated, a spirit came, and I agreed to go with the experience it would bring me but first I called to the Coyote: "Do not desert me!" After a very long while, of things that have gone misty, an invisible Being fed me some strawberries from a spoon. As I took them in my mouth and ate them, the very vibrant colour red travelled slowly down my body from top to bottom causing me to sweat and burn until I was completely red.

In one of the deep drops I had seen the colour blue; now the blue came and interwove with the red. Eventually they separated out so that red was below, and blue was above. Across the centre, through the solar plexus, was a band of clear crystal. In this crystal layer I came to rest my attention. The Ancient Grandfather came and, following him, came the Girl. I wanted to fix her image in my mind, but she began to withdraw down a long tunnel. Feeling: "That hasn't lasted very long!" I determined to follow her. She went down and down and down, and I went down and down and down, and when I came out of the tunnel she was gone, there was nothing, it was black. A spirit was there saying: "Let go." I listened and when I heard those words, I tried to liberate myself from the fears that hold me in place.

Finally, as the Owl, I found myself standing on a stretch of clean wet beach with rocks and cliffs to my left. The pebbles on this beach were round and flat and glistening, the light was black. The Girl appeared as if she had just been born, yes, she came riding by on a white horse. I flew to them, the Girl was sitting on a saddle made of wood, I perched on the horns of the saddle and we went forward.

### The Wake-up Call

As I came to consciousness from sleeping, I was aware of the presence of the Chief, Joseph's brother, Chief of the first Sun Moon Dance ceremony in the United Kingdom which I had recently participated in and there had become a Sun Moon dancer. I heard the Coyote say: "The Chief is going to show you the gift he gave you at the Sun Moon Dance." A process occurred in which I was tied to the Dance Tree at the level of my solar plexus with the four colours of the medicine wheel: Yellow, White, Black, and Red.

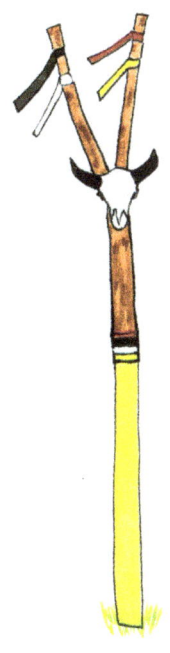

*the Dance Tree*

    In my vision I was tied facing the Y-shaped Tree with my arms up, like the two branches. My head was where the buffalo skull was hanging at the place where the trunk becomes two and I experienced sneaking up on the browsing herd, no horses, sneaking up on them and stabbing them in the neck, the red blood pouring out and covering us, the hunters. The buffalo trying to get up, shuddering and dropping dead and we would lie there, close to our dead bison. The herd, being unaware of the cause of these deaths, moved on, and we skinned and used every part of those we had killed.

    I don't know if this ever happened, but it is a metaphor of taking what you need without disturbing everything else. Yes, there was something very ok about that way of killing; it was sacrificial, dangerous, took us to the limits of our skill and safety, and kept us alive.

In the time that I was at the Tree I understood how it was that the bones of the Ancient Grandfather fell into me and what the impression of him hung up by his shoulders was, although, in my case, I was facing the Tree. He was facing the other way. Hum, I am having a clear impression of the intensely metaphoric nature of all these experiences. Oh, I am facing towards the Tree because I am going in for the knowing, and he was hung with his back to the Tree because he had the knowing which he was passing on.

This was the gift. Thank you, Chief!

Here I am in Scotland, at the Findhorn Foundation, attending a week-long seminar led by my Teacher. The seminar is called *Shamanic Consciousness*, and during the week we will take altered-state journeys to gather experiences.

I arrived the day before the course was due to begin and, after attempting in a half-hearted fashion to find a bed and breakfast place, I pitched my tent on the campsite adjacent to the seminar venue and went out walking, praying, trying to get myself into the correct place ready for the week's work, and I got the feeling that everything was fine, I just had to wait.

Lying in my tent that night I meditated, I was at the starting line of a race track and all the four medicine wheel colours were there. I was looking at them confusedly: "Which one is the starting flag?" Suddenly they all moved at once and a voice shouted: "Go!" ......... the race was on.

*the starting flag*

Next morning, I struck my tent and went to register, moving into the provided accommodation with three other people on the course. We all got on ok, but towards the end of the first day I found myself getting the most horrendous headache. It was something to do with, or rather, it wasn't helped by, being too close to other people, and I thought maybe I should move, move from the bedroom that I have on my own, that I like very much, that is very cosy, and very pleasant. The sacred things I have arranged in there are in perfect positions, it feels good, but I am not supposed to be in that comfortable situation! However, I spent that first night there.

I remember one image from the night. All the colours of the medicine wheel had come to me. The colours were very, very strong and brilliant and had changed me radically. When I woke up this morning the headache was so bad that I was going to throw up. There were four of us in the bungalow, where the walls were paper thin and there was only one loo. So, I went out into the nearby dunes and threw up violently there. Then I lay face down and, connecting my energy centres to the earth, tried to get better. Slowly during the day, I have got better but I am still extremely wobbly.

It is a good job I got sick for no apparent reason at the Sun Moon Dance (on the first day I was very, very sick, but that's another story), otherwise I bet I'd be looking for all sorts of reasons why I got sick here. One of them would be a large woman on the course with her dominant and unsubtle personality pushing her way into my psychic envelope. At the end of the session last night this woman became extremely enthusiastic about the fact that I looked like 'a Red Indian'. She declared she could see it in me, and she thought it was a previous incarnation. I, on the other hand, thought to myself that it was more likely a channelling kind of phenomenon, especially when someone else said they could see three native american spirits in the room.

Maybe inspired by this conversation, when I came to meditate, I saw the tall, straggly-haired Grandfather and I invoked him with prayer: "Grandfather, whose bones are my bones, teach me! Grandfather, whose bones are in me, teach me! Grandfather, whose bones are mine, teach me!" Those were the variations on the theme, and during the experience I occasionally repeated them, especially if my concentration was about to waver. I was conscious enough to know that teachings came, but they arrived in an incomprehensible form and entered my body with some pain.

After a while I found that my inner eyes were blindfolded. The Grandfather had put a blindfold on me, and he wanted me not to try and see. I could sense his presence and I concentrated on that. My lower energy centres began to have feeling. My generative centre revolved in an anticlockwise direction in a most gentle way, and deeply sensitive and loving energy expressed itself there. The energy moved up to the solar plexus where it revolved clockwise. It ascended in a vertical column into my heart and burned and infused my heart centre. Then it began to rise again, but it seemed to be going to bypass my throat, and I made a decision to go and see what was happening in the throat centre. I found that there was a garrotte, a ligature, something that was thin and pale yellow like a buckskin strip, tied around this throat centre pulling it to the back. I understood that the Grandfather was strangled with a garrotte and the throat centre was silenced. There was no shock, no horror, with that, it just was the fact. Then the feeling of the Grandfather came over me and slowly that image of the throat centre faded away. From there I came back, into a very calm and peaceful state. I have moved from sharing accommodation with others and being on my own is easier for me.

The minute the drumming started the Black Coyote appeared like a whirlwind and knocked me sideways, out of my body to the left. Although it took me completely by surprise, I accepted his tornado arrival, and he took me down through a series of vortices which were on the left-hand side of my body; one, two, three vertically down, and then along a more horizontal one that cut into my body and made all of my lower centres jump. This altered my state profoundly and we went into complete blackness, travelling together very closely, with him leading the way.

It was a long dark journey during which I experienced physical ecstasy. I found I could do amazing things with my body. I could open it up and see and feel the thousands of folds that went right the way down the front, all billowing and flapping like fronds of tall seaweed in the darkness of the blackness, layers upon layers unfolding to be felt and seen.

After a long while, we came to a world where some blue circular patterns were visible on the ground. When I bent down in the gloom to have a close look, I found that these were black pebbles; some very small amount of light was reflecting off them and that is how they appeared to be blue. Still crouching down, I looked along the beach, the scene was familiar, and I felt sure I had once met the Girl and the Horse here. I looked up and there they were, standing by a large rock. Moving ahead of the Coyote I went towards them. Coming up to the Girl, I stepped into her and we became as one person. We travelled, and we entered a sandy desert that was flat for as far as the eye could see.

We looked around; there was nothing to see. A conference followed between the three of us, White Horse, Girl with Red Ribbons and Black Coyote, because something was missing. It was a something with the quality of yellowness. We decided we would look for this yellowness, and we wanted to find a golden-yellow sphere. We knew the size of sphere we were searching for, the diameter of which would have been from the level of my eyes to my navel. The three of us stood in a circle and we wondered how we could find anything in this desert where there was nothing but sand. I expected one of us to have the answer, but it became an endless think-tank of how to proceed. Going around in circles, the discussion lasted for aeons. We were stuck in an endless loop. We were completely stuck.

So, faced with complete inability to achieve the goal we set ourselves, we began to compromise, and we said: "Yes, so, well, ok then, this sand is made of millions of golden-yellow spheres, so let's choose one of those." ........ But which one? How to make a choice? And this became even more distressing because there were billions and billions of grains of sand and in what way would you choose between one and the other? And how would you ever construct a system to find the one that you wanted? How would you ever know it was the right one? We were overcome by choice and another state of extraordinary stuck-ness took over, only very slightly different to the one before.

I thought hard, because this sphere was a symbol in my meditative life that belonged to somebody important: "Who was it that owned a golden sphere?" After a long struggle, I remembered that the golden sphere belonged to the Yellow Coyote. As soon as I had that thought the Yellow Coyote erupted out of the sand like a dust devil. Creating his own vortex, many grains of sand were attracted to him as he rose from the desert floor and many grains of sand were falling from him as he shook his body into shape. He shouted at us, not in anger, more in exasperation, and he said: "What does it matter if it is one grain or a million? I can make myself out of any grain here, or I can choose a thousand grains, or a million, and I can make myself out of all these grains of sand into any size I want." And he began to grow and grow and grow, and that was magnificent to watch. I mean, I would have been quite happy if for the rest of the journey the Coyote had just grown out of the vast desert into the hugest, hugest, hugest creature that I had ever seen. But suddenly he vanished.

We were deserted, left looking at each other in a helpless kind of way. Less than helpful thoughts came my way and I looked impatiently at my companions thinking loudly to myself: "That white horse is completely redundant. I can't even imagine what it is doing here." Then I asked the girl: "What shall we do?" and she hopped from one foot to the other, like a little bird dancing. It was a pretty pathetic dance. It was quite obvious that it would achieve nothing, so, ignoring the Black Coyote, I said emphatically: "This place is finished. Let's go back to the place that we came from."

We retraced our steps back to the black pebbles where the light was black. I turned to the Black Coyote and I affirmed that I did trust him completely and I understood that I would be with him while he was teaching me something that was extremely hard, and that I would try my best to depend upon him. I said: "You allowed me to follow that phantasy, so I could learn from it. I know it is a lesson about the nature of time and choice. How points of time are like a desert of sand and there is no choice to be made between one or another point of time, or any difference between them. That the greatest thing I can do or achieve is either in one point in time or a million and I have got those millions of points of time. But why make a choice and how would that choice be made? So,": I said, drawing breath: "if that is the lesson there, I will follow you now." And he said: "Yes, follow me." In fact, after I had said all that I think he smiled at me encouragingly and said: "Well, now follow me."

We entered into completer darkness. Darkness without vortices, darkness without feelings, darkness without movement, without excitement, without a sense of purpose, and I began to get suffocated. I thought: "I am starting to panic." I asked the Black Coyote to come closer to me because I trusted him, and he was all I had. My breathing was eased by bringing him closer and, after a moment, I found that the back of my body was opening up just like the cargo doors on the bottom of an aeroplane. As we exited through my open back the suffocating feeling stopped, and we entered a place that was formless; there was no pressure either, it was a no-thing place, and that is where we stayed. I listened to the drum, which held me together; otherwise I would have fallen apart.

When the drumming changed to call us back, I depended entirely on the Coyote because I could not have returned. The Black Coyote brought me back and, on the way, I saw that sterile desert that only the Yellow Coyote could make sensible, it looked like an offshoot of a root, or, perhaps, the appendix.

We were nearly back when I asked anxiously: "What happened to the vortices on the way back?" The Coyote laughed and said: "The vortices are only on the way down. Your consciousness has changed, and you won't go back through them unless you returned to the same place which you won't do."

We arrived back, and I came out of that trip as fast as I could. I had no desire to re-live or dwell in any of it, but I knew perfectly well that it was engraved in my memory in such a way that I wouldn't forget it. The experiences, in the blackness and the darkness, of the strange capabilities of my body have not diminished, but what can they mean to me? Luckily, to some extent, the unbearable intensities of the difficulties in the sand desert have gone. Yes, and some of the overwhelming feeling of the no-thing-ness has also gone. But I felt very serious and silent and detached when I came back. Someone in the group asked a question. That brought me back to life and I saw this world as quite a treasured place to be because it has infinite variety in it and all the parts of it seemed to me like precious dinky toys.

We had the afternoon off. I slept, travelled, and got lost on the astral plain for a couple of hours. Then I went out for a walk. As I walked, I thought of how I loved horses when I was a child, how I desperately wanted a horse, the disappointment, the anger I felt at my parents because they would not let me have one when I felt it would have been easy as we lived on a farm. I had not thought of this for years and years. Now I realized that the Girl with the Red Ribbons was me.

When I merged with her in the journey I was surprised because I wanted to promote her, not be her. I had thought she was connected to Joseph's work. That is an amusing thing to say because I too am connected to that work. Anyway, it came home to me that I was the girl who danced, not expertly, but with feeling. Then it came home more because I realized that the day I broke my arm, when I was ten years old, and ceased to have a future as a professional dancer I was wearing the colour red. I was wearing a red skirt which was the costume for the gypsy dance we were rehearsing at that time. I was so fond of it, I wore it constantly....... Well, now that I remember, I notice a long story in my life full of details that correspond with these unexpected experiences.

When I meditated one morning during the seminar, I'm jumping back in time now, I came to consciousness in the middle of a conversation where I was talking to someone about what I like and dislike. A spirit voice said to me: "You are still asleep." That statement has been with me constantly since then, and, standing by the river yesterday, near the place where two streams meet, I stated, to whatever spirits were listening, the fact that I don't know how to wake up, but there was no reply. It seems that I have to find the way for myself.

So, this morning as I lay down to enter an altered state, I felt a spirit present, very calm and very quiet. I began to sing: "Help me, please help me!" ............ In response to this request the spirit opened my solar plexus and this was a figure of eight, sea-rolling movement. Then my heart centre opened, a still circle where the energy concentrated itself and seemed to gain mass. Then the meditative eye, where the perception would enter in and the thought process would go out, although the interchange between them was so smooth that there was simply a sensation of being able to see seamlessly. After a while, I realized that these three places, solar plexus, heart and eyes, breathe, in and out; that breath is even a function of the eyes, the eyes breathe; all the energy centres breathe.

I found the Coyotes to be close; they were very, very small so I needed to hold onto them tightly, and I took them, one in each hand. I remembered the details of the desert journey. I remembered how the back of my spinal column had opened and the Black Coyote had taken me into the void. What a radical shift it was to perceive and to enter the void. I opened my spinal column and moved to find the entrance again, but I heard that the centre moves. Yes, the centre, the entrance to the void, is never in the same place; it has no placement.

The image of the straggly-haired Grandfather whose bones are in me came, and he became the entrance. He held me, so that I didn't vanish, and I went in. I discovered that I could move a little, and I found that if I put the Coyotes into my eyes I could see, if I put them into my ears I could hear, if I put them into my nostrils I could smell, and if I held them in my hands I could feel. The mouth is different, because in every other case there are two openings to place the contraries in order to perceive but in the mouth, there is only one: ears, two holes; eyes, two holes; nose, two holes; hands, two holds; mouth, one. There's a perception I can't quite grasp, but, if there is only one opening to the void and it moves, maybe the mouth is the entrance to the void.

In this void experience I didn't feel the challenging ego-feelings that I had in the desert part of the recent journey, but I did feel some very radical changes of consciousness which have made me very calm, then and do now, even so, during the return, there was a lot of pain. I lay here, not happy, and my body was closing, except for a split down the front which felt like it had a knife buried in it. The image of my Teacher came and hovered above this split and brought me back into an enjoyment of this place of daily life, and I suddenly realised the importance of the living Teacher. I previously thought that the living Teacher opened the gates to other worlds, but this morning I completely appreciated that they also give the student a reason for returning to this world by the fact that they also inhabit a physical body. That was a new understanding for me on why it is so important to have a living Teacher when starting this radical work.

So, I thank the Coyotes, the Grandfather, and my living Teacher, for helping me on this journey, and I realize that I have to learn to cope with the dynamics that are going on in my everyday life and accept these clear, clear spaces when they arrive; accept them as a great gift, enjoy them, and allow them to enter my daily life too.

### The Name of the Grandfather

Well, back at home I have entered turmoil again. Today the many mistakes of someone at work were very aggravating. She was unusually dense and didn't listen to what I said to her. Worse than this, yesterday after an order arrived the customer rang up and told me that she had never placed an order; that my partner had promised an estimate and when it didn't come, she had gone elsewhere. I felt sick and I wondered why I ever bothered to try and delegate anything. Now I just feel despair and a desire not to have to run my business any more.

Last night I had some very powerful experiences, particularly of riding a horse. At the end the two Coyotes came and stabilized me, placing the heart centre around my whole Being, and, in that state, they encouraged me to look at the work situation again, which I found I was able to do without negative feelings, but I knew I wanted out, badly wanted out.

I tried to remember who was the spirit with me when the horse came, who encouraged me? It was the straggly-haired Grandfather, and I had a very long and intense contact with him. It was he who encouraged me to experience all the power of the white horse which is in my lower centres but will carry me to the upper world.

When I shut my eyes to meditate this morning the horse was there, not as a visual image, but as a surrounding essence of the whiteness of its body. I felt the spirits encouraging me and I changed my state of being to lie within and appreciate the power of the horse from within. It struck me as ironic because I thought that I would ride this horse something like a normal rider, but I found that the riding of the horse that I was to do was an internal understanding of the energy of the horse. That was the way that the spirit world could move my consciousness into a place of receptivity, so this was a very different sort of riding.

There was a great change. I sank into the darkness of the blackness and I realized that I was entering the earth. The internal body of Mother Earth is a strange substance that resembles the depths of the sea. I began to sing the sound of carrying, the sound '-uu', and the golden sphere was clearly visible in the void. I said to myself: "I have reached the Uu-sphere." I knew exactly what the Uu-sphere was. It was perfection, completeness, appreciation of the vast self within the non-existence.

Yes, and from that appreciation I began to see the Sun Moon Dance Tree. In particular, I saw the chip from the trunk of that Tree where a small branch had been taken off while we were preparing it for the Dance; the chip was a pale-yellow sliver with a hole, where the branch had been, in the centre. I had kept it and brought it home. This knot-hole from the Tree became the sound '-uu' and the Ancient Grandfather came in a process that involved the opening of my back into an awareness until he was very present.

Looking at him I realized that the knot-hole I brought home from the Tree is a symbol of the Grandfather. The sound '-uu' and the wind blowing out of the darkness of the void belong to him. I prayed to him: "Thank you, thank you, Grandfather." This is how I did it, I whispered: "Grandfather, Grandfather, Grandfather, Grandfather." And I said: "Thank you, thank you, thank you, you came to me, and I am coming to you." Meaning that the effort was on both sides and I wasn't just some chosen object. I, in my own power, was willing to come to the Grandfather, and he wanted me to come to him. I wondered what his name was and, seeing the hollow portion of the Dance Tree, I said: "hollow", the word 'hollow' was yellow. The word 'oak' came, and it was red. I said: "hollow oak tree", the word 'tree' was grey. Those were the colours; yellow, red, and grey, and they were the colours of the Ancient Grandfather. I said: "That is the name, Hollow Oak Tree, '-Oh-oh-oh-ii'. Becoming teachable many times expands awareness; that is the name." And I came back feeling good, as if I had achieved a lot.

As I lay here, I was aware of my spirit body outside my physical one. I don't know, I suppose I am doing well enough for a human being, I just hope that I am doing well enough in this process, and that everything is going all right.

### Help is the Colour Yellow

I began to become aware of the straggly-haired Grandfather. I began to call to him: "Grandfather whose bones are in me, help me! Grandfather whose bones are mine, help me! Grandfather, whose bones are my bones, help me!" I became entirely aware of this grey-haired Grandfather, and with him came that pale-yellow colour. I saw my Teacher's leather medicine bag which is also that colour; it was as if the Grandfather was inside the medicine bag. I saw his face very clearly, long and angular with deep furrows, and I saw his greyness; he is the Ancient Grandfather.

When I was completely helped by this Grandfather, and help is the colour yellow; as I say the word, I see that colour; the Owl hooted outside. This started a process in me, and I became the Owl. Yes, I became the Owl, there was a complete amalgamation of my psyche with it and I became it. I flew as the Owl to the shoulder of the Ancient Grandfather, then to his hand where I picked up one of his thumb bones. I felt that my mission was to fly all his bones into the darkness and I asked him to guide me.

As he entered me, my solar plexus knotted up and I knew there would be some powerful activity. The colour red flushed through; a complete surrender was required of my rational mind and this I did. I carefully cleared my mind and did not allow any self-generated images to dominate. Eventually my meditative eye and my lower eye, the solar plexus, were open. They looked upwards and an entirely new thing happened whereby the light beams from these two eyes crossed at a certain point way above my horizontal body, and where they crossed a diamond star was illuminated and it twinkled in the sky.

I realized that my perception had changed, and a new dimension had been added. A pyramid-shaped crystal was now my perception tipped by the diamond star, and I was able to enter into this pyramid and be there. Within the pyramid the throat centre was entirely clear and open, and that is how the Ancient Grandfather was able to come to me so strongly. After a long time of moving together, after I had said prayers, he gave me one of his longest bones, the right upper leg bone. This yellow bone lay in my body and I considered the function of this bone in the body, considered how it is the vertical strength of the leg, a weight bearing bone for the entire upper body, how it is stability and movement. I learnt a lot from this bone.

Then I saw myself as a young person and the Grandfather was teaching me. We were standing in front of a lodge, the square door of which was made by three poles. He said: "Shall we go in?" We stepped in; the lodge was white inside and bore a likeness to the crystal pyramid. In my hand I had a seed. I pushed the two halves against each other and I heard the sound as the skin of this bean-shaped seed split. I looked at the little comma of the sprout of the seed that was inside. Putting the two halves back together, I planted this seed in the very centre of my Being. I wondered whether that seed would grow after I had split it. I had the understanding that the splitting of that seed was to show me that I am only half complete and that I must complete and be whole.

After this insight I was lying in the recovery position not recovering when I realized that I was in a crystal body and not my physical body. Something moved to the left above, it hit the crystal body and golden light came out like a puff of smoke, somehow in that way, I got back into my own body and came fully back here.

These are psychic states I am describing, and out in the travelling state sometimes the experience is painful. At those times I may want to force myself back to normal consciousness, but I know that would be foolhardy and, by doing it, the least I would lose would be what I was trying to perceive. When the pain happens, I ask for help and stay with what is happening. Help is never long in coming.

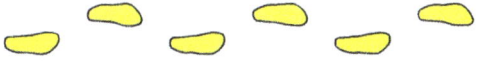

I came to meditate, and I saw again my Teacher's pale-yellow medicine bag. I saw that the energy of the Grandfather is held within the Sun Moon Dance bag and the Ancient Grandfather came to me. He came into my whole Being, and this is where I am going to start to lose bits, but he came, and I became completely aware of him as I have experienced him before, so that I intimately know his colours: yellow, red, and grey. Then he focused my attention in yellow and grey; the grey separated into its component colours, black and white, the white then disappeared and the two remaining colours became the black and yellow symbols of the energy centres, symbols which had been developing in my awareness for some time.

8 energy centres in a body:

top of the head
meditative eye
throat centre
heart centre
solar plexus
navel centre
generative centre
root centre

In this way I understood the origin of those symbols and I found myself standing between the two lights: black and yellow. A tall, narrow stemmed, red goblet with a shallow cup was visible there; I became the stem of that goblet. Within the stem was a black space that I could enter. I entered into a semicircular cavern inside the protection of the Grandfather. I stood on the flat floor of that cavern, but I knew that below it a perfect circle was completed by another semicircular space which was very different to the black space that existed within me.

At the centre of the semicircle that I was standing in there was half a black box. The other half of the black box was below, in a safer place, with some connection to the black cavern above by which one could descend. I began to descend that vertical shaft very slowly. I was nervous and a rope, like the rope of a church bell, appeared beside me and I held onto that as I descended. When I reached the bottom of the rope, the pit went further; I had to let go and fall to the ground, but in this black space movement was very slow and very easy, only done by thought, and nothing could hurt me. There were no falls and no precipices and, afraid as I had been of it, there was no fear. I landed, and I heard the sentence: "How long can the human mind dwell on emptiness?"

I held the black space for a while. Eventually I recalled a prayer I once made: "I bring my light to the dark space" and so I brought it there. It took the form of a golden kidney-shaped seed and I laid it down on the black ground of the emptiness where it looked like a golden pebble emitting its own light. The memory of the Grandfather's yellowed bones returned to me. The second bone of the big toe of the left foot was one that was specifically shown to me today.

Then there was a change, and I found the Dance Tree coming towards my energy centres. I was wide open, and the Tree entered. I saw that in the distant past the Grandfather died at a ceremonial dance, garrotted on the Tree. Then I saw that the spiritual instructions for the Sun Moon Dance, given to Joseph Rael in the 1980s, had brought a new dance ceremony to men and women of all races, and that, by dancing together, an opportunity was created to change the energy of our world. Those are the insights that came to me today about the Grandfather and he is now the Grandfather of the Dance Tree, if such a title exists.

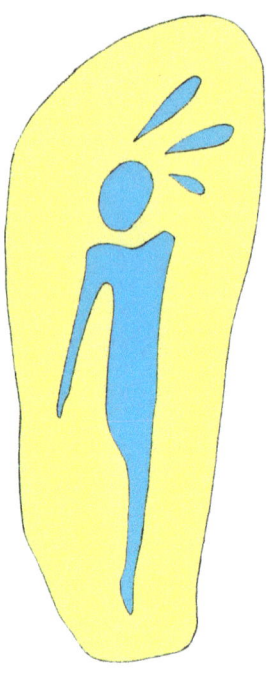

*the Grandfather in the Tree*

Again last night, I dreamed of Joseph who brought the Sun Moon Dance to us.

The Buffalo was present, red ties were on one horn and blue on the other. I felt the snorting of his breath and the colour green seemed to emanate from his nostrils. I entered the big brown form; this process took a very, very long time and I can't really say how many changes of state happened there. There were many give-aways and openings and acceptances required on my part in order to be there, all of which I am willing to do, but my lifetime programming occasionally gets in the way.

After entering completely into the psyche of the Buffalo, a hole opened up in front of me and I was overcome by the feeling that I was going to enter the digestive system. This I really did not want to do and yet I knew that if it was the next thing that had to be done,

I should do it. I called the Coyotes and they came strongly and helped me to go on.

A shaft led downwards, and I descended. Reaching the bottom, I came into a village. The houses were leather-covered mounds with straight poles at the doors. In the middle of the village was a huge Tree. I went straight to the Tree. I lingered there; I didn't hurry on, I allowed its magnetism to slowly draw me in. I went into the golden-yellow interior of the Tree and the place I entered contained the Ancient Grandfather.

A little voice said: "I, I, I...." That was me hanging on to my ego and I knew I must stop it. Appreciating the Grandfather, I began to say: "You, you, you...." Although better, this was not quite correct. I said: "We, we, we...."

When I was completely 'we' with the Grandfather he bent down and began to dig into a bank. He pulled a creature out from the ground, a brown, squirming, screaming creature who was expending lots of energy to divert my attention. The peculiar sound it made caused my mind to slip, and a voice said to me very gently: "Concentrate on the nature Being." I focused on it again. It was screaming and writhing as if the Grandfather were trying to kill it. He uncurled it, a bit like a hedgehog, and did something to it. Then, putting it back into the ground again, he let it go.

I began to come back through a lot of things that .... have gone. I tried to think, afterwards, what this journey was all about, and I feel that in the experience is the reason why I am important. I am important because I am incarnate here. I don't know why I should need to be there to see that, but the very deep feelings I had all the way through were that it was the right thing to be doing even though it didn't suit my ego particularly well. At one point I remember saying: "Is it really like this?" Something was happening that was so peculiar it could not enter my memory, and I just had to accept this and let it go.

# Gifts from the Southern Hemisphere

In the last days of October 1999 my Teacher, who had been Joseph's student since the 1980s, and I travelled from the UK to Australia. I danced in the first Sun Moon Dance to be held in that continent. Joseph, Beautiful Painted Arrow, was Chief there and I had the opportunity to meet him for the first time. After the ceremony was over, my Teacher and I hired a car and travelled to the Red Centre to visit the largest rock on Earth, Uluru.

The Grandfather called me, and I listened to him. He called an Eagle and I remembered how the Eagle came in visions in the night after the first evening visit my Teacher and I made to the greatest rock. This took me back to the Sun Moon Dance when Wedge-tailed Eagles came to fly around the arbour as we put up the Tree, and, during the Dance, from my place at the West gate, I saw one swooping across the scrubland, undercarriage down, feet extended to strike, and this sight made a deep impression on me.

On Sunday, in the late morning, the Chief had stopped the dancing. He pointed to me and said: "You will take the White ribbon, the colour of the South, from the Tree. Take it, and carry it, and bring it back next year." Thoughts jumped up in my mind: "Oh, I have to come back next year! I did not intend to come again. Oh, it is so far!" But before these thoughts were finished others said: "This is the colour White! There are aeroplanes. It doesn't take so long to get here. This is the colour White!" I knew that my connection to the colour White was going to be established and I was deeply grateful for this gift. I danced slowly, as instructed, to the Tree and receiving the White ribbon that was tied around the trunk, I tied it around my neck in deference to the Grandfather. Then the Chief turned to another woman and gave her the custodianship of the Yellow. She danced to the Tree and received the yellow ribbon. Later in the day he gave the Black and Red ribbons to two of the men in the same way.

There were many dancers, even so at times the path to the Tree was completely clear, but at those times I never got the call to go. Then, sometime on Sunday afternoon, my solar plexus began to heave and stretch itself towards the Tree. My arms went numb to the elbows, I was panting, and I was longing to smash myself against the Tree. Suddenly everybody seemed to be in the centre. I was dancing backwards and forwards on one spot praying for an opening because I was going to explode. Suddenly a small gap appeared, and I went through. I hit the Tree and fell. I hit the ground without any feeling of pain or any sensation in my body; I just heard a tremendous thump and the ground shook. They picked me up and carried me out of the arbour into the women's tipi.

Lying there I became aware of the presence of a Spirit of enormous size which filled my visual field and all my perception. I spoke out boldly and I told that Spirit that I was awake. Listening to myself I found it quite shocking because in what way was I awake? I didn't appear to have woken up, or to have any sense of a radical change of consciousness. There was no blinding flash, or sudden increase in awareness, but I did say: "I am awake" while my shocked little self thought: "Oh, I ...., I have said this, and so now I must realize it."

After visiting Uluru, still travelling in Australia, I began to record my meditations again in a sporadic fashion. One morning I met Joseph and through him I came to the Ancient Grandfather. The Grandfather gave me all the bones of his spine and he said that I had done well, and I deserved a gift. We went into a shop. He asked me what I would like. My conscious brain went into overdrive and I could not think what I would like. There was a blank moment. When I came to, I was putting a wooden pipe into the zip pocket of a green bag. It was a musical pipe, not a smoking pipe, made of cedar wood and played like a recorder. This was the gift.

A week or so later, when I was staying with a friend near Brisbane, we visited a place called Rainbow Beach. As we walked along the street, I noticed an art shop and suggested we went in to have a look around. We found there some beautifully made hand drums. I was busy trying these when my eye was caught by some wooden pipes on a high shelf. I picked one and I bought both a pipe and a drum. The desire for a drum had long been present in my consciousness, but the idea of the pipe came directly from the Grandfather, and I take the musical pipe to be his special gift.

Back at home in England, as I started to meditate one morning, I got the smallest inkling of the Grandfather and I called out: "Grandfather, Grandfather, Grandfather," and tried to move towards a closer appreciation of him. My throat centre opened, and I saw a blue spot of light there. I travelled towards that light and put all my concentration into it. This worked, and slowly I came closer and closer to the Grandfather until I met him and found myself sitting in the multi-coloured sands of Rainbow Beach. Joseph was there too, sitting in a four-wheel drive vehicle, and I was asking him if he had a job for me when I remembered that he had given me the White ribbon to carry and that was my job. I felt some force coming from far away. It entered my generative centre and energised it. This force was the colour white and from that point the colour white took my consciousness and filled me with white. The colour White, the colour of the South in Joseph's teaching; the medicine wheel direction whose attribute is placement.

I asked the Grandfather: "What is placement?" In reply he infused me with the colour green. I strained to listen, and I worked out this: "With your thoughts you make the world." I moved further towards the Grandfather, and I began to puzzle: "So how can I make a peaceful world?" He came as the colour yellow against the colour green that was me, and I saw him die on the ceremonial Tree. I asked: "Isn't this a bit like Jesus Christ?" I questioned this vision because the teaching that Jesus' death takes away the sins of the world is a belief I can't accept. I can't accept that a person's sin can be taken away by somebody else, and it seemed to me that the Grandfather's death might be similar. That is why I said: "Isn't this death a bit like Jesus Christ?" After a little while I heard this: "There is no greater love than this: that a man should lay down his life for another." And I understood the teaching a different way: that it is the emanation of love into the world that counts, not whether people are exonerated from their sin.

Then my eye of seeing opened. I walked forwards through my meditative eye into a dark space. The journey became very painful and difficult because I entered this space alone. I was afraid, and thought I should surrender my consciousness, thought that this was what was required of me, that this was the great give-away. But when I tried to do it, I couldn't achieve it and I heard: "That is not what is wanted." The encouraging thought came to me: "They don't want me to give up my consciousness!" So I pressed forward with my consciousness despite the pain and the illness, and I have to say that I wanted to give up, but where was there that I wanted to go back to? With the Grandfather encouraging me to go forward I went into the formless nothingness darkness of somewhere. I don't know where it was, but it was not nice to be there. In that pain and difficulty, I pulled myself forwards so that even the connection with the Grandfather was lost. In that terrible state I waited.

At some point the perception came to me: "I am light" and I realized that I, on my own, completely alone in the darkness of the dreadful place to which, encouraged by the spirits, I had dragged myself, was the light, and with my thoughts I made light. I felt that by entering that place I had contributed to peace in the world. I began to feel myself coming back. I came back through all the stages. At one point the spirits greeted and congratulated me, and there were many of them. Then I came to the Coyote and back into my body.

I woke up at four in the morning, perfectly alert, and couldn't go back to sleep. My solar plexus was knotted up, and eventually I realized that I should meditate, so, at about four thirty, I did. The knot very soon eased away. After a while Joseph appeared; he said something to me like: "As long as you're working for me so and so and such and such shall be the case." But I have completely forgotten what he said. This convinces me that I really did connect to him because it is similar to when he teaches me in life, half of what he says vanishes from my memory without trace. Nevertheless, deep transformations take place.

So, I don't remember how it came about that he showed me how I was the wooden pipe which I had bought in Australia. He showed me that there are nine holes on the pipe. There is the entrance hole of the breath going in and there is the final exit hole of the remaining breath going out. There is an air hole surrounded by the bridge and there are six finger holes. That makes nine. He showed me that the energy centre at the top of my head is the hole over which the bridge of the pipe can be adjusted to create and channel the quality of the sound. Played with the fingers of the left-hand, the next hole is the meditative eye, next the throat, then the heart. Played by the right-hand then come the solar plexus, the navel centre, and the generative centre. The root centre is the place where the remaining air leaves the hollow stem. That makes eight.

While this made good sense to me as a working metaphor, I was puzzled as to what the metaphor of the first hole is. Ah, it is the place where the spirit breath comes in, and the eight remaining holes are the holes in my body where the power animals manifest themselves. They manifest themselves like the wind rushing through the holes in the pipe. Wait, now I remember what Joseph said: "While you are working for me it will always be like this, that you are the hollow pipe and spirit plays its tune through you."

Then the pipe went limp and became a snake and I saw the image of Uluru, in the Red Centre of Australia, entering into my centre of generation.

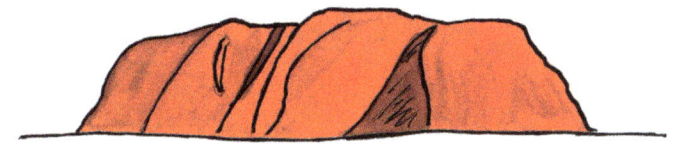

*Uluru*

I saw the pythoness, whose name is Kuniya, come out of the rock, and I realized that I had now to learn about the power of the snake. On all the native paintings of the python that I saw at Uluru white eggs were hung round her neck like beads on a necklace. I thought: "What is the point of these eggs? Are they ideas that are to be carried and given birth to through the body of this work?" I didn't know the answer to this, but I knew that the power of the snake had to be understood through the generative centre and I was reluctant to start that work. I seem to recall that Joseph said: "It doesn't matter if you start it now or later because it is inevitable that you will start it and it will be done." So, I am nervous, and I don't know how the snake teachings are going to work out.

###  Opening the Gates

I was straining at the limits of my ability today. At first, I was quietly travelling through a series of sensations, which I do call body sensations but the answer as to their exact nature and location is a mystery, when I entered the Tree. I inched my way forward through the inner body of the Tree feeling, oh, joyful, enlivened, activated.

Suddenly I found myself standing on the viewing platform that looks towards Kata Tjuta which is about forty kilometres west of Uluru in the Red Centre of Australia. As I looked the rocks began to travel towards me in a most extraordinary fashion, Kata Tjuta was moving.

*Kata Tjuta*

I allowed this to happen in quite a state of surprise. Eventually I was overwhelmed, and I entered into the centre of a particular rock. Slowly, out of the rock itself, a snake emerged: I was going to learn right there about the power of the snake.

I saw a Python so enormous it encircled the Earth and, squeezing the life out of the world, digested it all. The idea came to me that as the snake absorbed everything it came to know everything. If you entered the power of the snake you would know everything. The Python was draped around my neck and I asked myself if I wanted to know everything. I am sure I did not want to, but the Grandfather was encouraging me to go forward.

He seemed to hang over me and I was, not exactly overawed, but I was full of grateful humility. I lay down on my belly on the ground in front of him. He took two small snakes and laid them on my back on either side of my spinal column and stamped them in. These snakes were small, stretching perhaps from the centre of my shoulder blades to not beyond my waist, and they were pale-yellow in colour. They each grew one green wing, which I suppose you could say would correspond roughly to the size of the shoulder blade. It struck me as very peculiar that one wing would be any use at all to a snake, but I think the idea was that the two snakes only function as a pair.

The Grandfather told me that I should play the pipe as a regular practice, and things have gone a bit hazy after that. When I eventually began to slowly withdraw from that deep place I felt extremely spaced out, ill, and at the limit of my energy. Suddenly

I sang a short song out loud. It burst out spontaneously for about four phrases, then I became conscious and finished it consciously, which, I must tell you, was not as good.

I found myself back here feeling pretty devastated that my daily life was going to now begin, but also with some relief because I had felt so extraordinarily peculiar out there at the limits of my perception. Hum, there was a name for out there. Yes, the Cave of the Ancestors, that's where I went when Kata Tjuta engulfed me. That cave is where the Snake resides.

No input during the night. I came to meditate, and, for a while, a very strange thing happened which was that the meditation progressed and at the same time I thought about where I was going to go shopping and how I was going to organize the day. Although this was working quite well, I became very angry with myself for not being able to concentrate on one thing.

The colour White began to arrive from the left-hand side, about my shoulder height and above. I took the colour White right into the centre of my body core and felt so happy to have it flooding my Being. Then I noticed the Yellow Coyote completely present below my waist to the right and the Black Coyote below my waist to the left. The final medicine wheel colour to arrive was the Red. This was deep below in the centre. I felt my lower centres begin to circle in a clockwise direction and, slowly, slowly, the Ancient Grandfather arrived. The feeling of his grandfather-ness became more and more evident until eventually we were joined together. When we were completely united the image of the hollow tree came to me and that was his name.

I saw the hollow wooden pipe and understood how important it is to play this pipe as a symbol of my connection with the Grandfather. Eventually, in the same place from which had emanated the colour White, a clear visual image of the Grandfather, fully clothed and standing upright, was visible. He was tall. His slightly bowed long legs and his entire body clad in beautiful pale-yellow buckskin clothes, both leggings and jacket with streamers hanging down. The image was so clear, it was time and it was necessary for me to change my brain waves. I did this and there was a complete change in the sound level inside my head; everything became very quiet and concentrated on one point. I stayed with that.

This one-point concentration was very intense and eventually I began to tire, so, rather than lose it through lack of concentration, I asked to come back and the Coyote came to help me. He brought with him a grey horse. I mounted and lay on the horse's back, sitting astride but slumped forward as if I had been through some great effort and was now shattered. I felt the power of the horse enter me and I allowed it to be. The horse became white and there was a blue streak down its back. The blue streak entered my body and changed my Being back to something with energy. I heard a word repeated: "Trust, trust, trust, trust." I did trust, the horse brought me back here and here I am.

This morning the Grandfather arrived and, changing my body awareness, he took me to a place I have never been before. It was very low down in my body to the left of my spinal column. In the physical body somewhere in the pelvic region, but in the spirit body miles and miles out into the darkness with only the impression of the spinal column far away as an indicator of the direction and the distance.

As I was moving in my awareness, he had told me that in this work there must be no inhibitions and no fear or it cannot be done. I felt how stupid I have often been to confuse the intense and ecstatic feelings of the spirit body with sexuality. To confuse them with sexual feelings is unhelpful and comes from the puritan streak in my christian culture.

I watched some colours there. I saw the colour blue as a point of disappearing light; it was like a meteor leaving its trail in the sky. As I watched this moving point of blueness, I became completely blue. A misty image of the white horse appeared. Remembering the Grandfather's comments, I approached the horse and rode it, rode it in that lower centre fashion which is so exciting. The blueness of my body attached itself with hooks into the body of the white horse so that we were as one.

I was thinking of the teaching that Joseph gave me in Australia: "Become the Power." It is a teaching I am working on and do not fully understand, nevertheless I feel that it must refer to a power beyond the personal, but, sat up on the horse's back, I felt I was becoming more and more myself in this powerful combination of blue and white.

Suddenly the horns of a Black Bull were present in my perception. The picture became clear and I found myself in the sandy arena of a white-painted bullring. I saw the colour green flaring in the nostrils of the bull and I knew that I had intended to kill him to release the red blood and the green power of growing from his body, but now I did not want to slaughter such a beautiful, powerful animal and I shouted: "Open the gates!"

As the gates opened the greatest expanse of green grass became visible, and I saw that there was no need to kill the bull to liberate the colour green because the green is freely available when you open the gates. I led the horse and the bull out of the enclosure, and we stood together on that great plain of grass.

I was struck by the fact that I was standing between the colours black and white and that all around us, for as far as the eye could see, the green was lushly growing and available. I thought: "Both the horse and the bull eat the green and only that. That is the only colour they need, then they just need some water and they are alive, but what about me? I can't survive in that way, so how am I going to live?" I feel pretty devastated by this now, but at the time I just thought: "That is not enough for me."

The Grandfather returned and took the picture away. I tried again to reach him in the realistic way that I saw him the other night and I prayed: "Grandfather, whose bones are my bones, help me! Grandfather, whose bones are in me, help me! Grandfather, who gave me your bones, help me!" Hearing it now I feel tears coming, but I wasn't emotional then. In response the Grandfather approached me, and he flooded me with the colour grey. I was thinking how much I hate the colour grey in everyday life, when he spoke this sentence: "You defeat yourself by your own expectations."

As the colour grey filled my perception from horizon to horizon, time ran out and the journey was over. I was unhappy that time in the world of everyday had called me back. I thanked the Grandfather, and I came back too fast because when I got here, I was in a state of mental distress at the thought of having to make the effort to record this journey. This happens sometimes, but the minute I pick the microphone up and start to speak that feeling of reluctance disappears. Even though I know this, it is often a tricky moment. However, if I record the journeys from the other place of consciousness then that is when static noise overwhelms the tape (ironically, when I typed up this section, I found that static had completely drowned out the next few sentences, so clearly, on this occasion, perhaps by returning too fast and alone, I had not managed the transition well).

When I came to meditate, I saw the golden sphere, the Uu-sphere. I have been confused and suffering from overload, so it was a relief to see this clear and beautiful sphere of energy resting in my centre of seeing. Then it moved down to my solar plexus. The colour green was appearing, and I knew I had to release some part of my psyche. I called the Black Coyote, I gave the parts of myself that I thought were not required into his keeping and returned to the centre of my Being.

A black cleft opened up down the entire length of my body. All sensation of pain was put to one side and this deep cleft became the focus of my attention. A large circular hole appeared beneath me, a hole with a grey misty atmosphere and no images. A great wind was blowing beneath this hole. The tips of my fingers were hanging onto the side of the great circle, one set touching the Black Coyote on the right, and other set the Yellow Coyote on the left, they said: "You will not fall, just let go and fly as the eagle." I looked down and I saw eagle's feet. After some hesitation I let go. As I dropped away from the hole I looked to see if there was a landscape, or anything, visible, but there was nothing, simply the colour grey, as if I was falling through cloud.

The essence of the Ancient Grandfather was present in the grey. I longed for him to be as close to me as I had seen him the other day. I glimpsed the pale-yellow buckskin of his clothes; I found him sitting on the grey horse and I went to the place where I really wanted to be, standing close, by the left shoulder of this beautiful animal, my right arm resting on its neck, my back against the leg of the Grandfather as he sat astride it. I hoped that he would put his hand on my shoulder, and he did. There was a deeply magical moment. Then he said to me kindly: "You must learn to love the things you hate." The fact that for so long I have hated the colour grey passed through my mind.

# Exploring the Grey

Last night was the seventh of January. It was the night for the fire ceremony, but it was impossible to hold it outside. Outside was howling wind and pouring rain. So, staying inside, I played the fire on the wooden pipe. I built the seven notes, or rather, I played the seven notes of the pipe, and I built the pile of twenty-eight sticks with them. I played striking the match and lighting the fire. I played the flames burning the pyre. The West side fell first, West, North, East, South, it burnt in that order, it fell in that order. Then I prayed to the Grandfathers and Grandmothers of the four directions. By visualizing my knowledge of these Ancestors, I made discoveries about which directions I have forged strong connections with and which I have not.

The following week I attended another seminar in Scotland, this one, called *Hands and Heart*, dedicated to learning spiritual healing. Our first journey would begin in a beautiful place in nature and we would journey on from there. But before the drumming started, my visual filed was full of the colour grey, elephant grey. It slowly dawned on me that I was in a cavernous place inside an elephant's head standing at the top of its trunk. The trunk was like a water shute formed from grey rock and I was sure that at the bottom of this shute there was a beautiful pool. When I exited the elephant's trunk, I would drop into this pool and see that I had just come down a beautiful waterfall. There would be a lovely sandy shore to sit on and beautiful nature all around. I thought: "That is good; maybe I will meet the Coyotes down there."

But suddenly the Coyotes were at the top of the trunk with me. They were in a very peculiar form, like cardboard cut-outs and small, standing on their hind legs they only reached up to between my knees and my waist. They were both there, identical, except that one was yellow, and one was black. I politely said hello to them, but they weren't so terribly keen to be sociable. Swiftly we decided to form a boat so that when the water would gush through, which would happen when the drumming started, we would fly down the waterfall as a boat and drop into the pool. So we sat: the black one at the front as the prow, I decided that would be good as he was the past, the yellow one behind me, as he is the future. I felt very pleased with this arrangement. It was quite logical: I can see my past, but I can't see my future.

When the drumming started there was no water, not even one trickle. I looked around, the cave we were in was formed by the skull of the elephant, and I could see two portals above us which were the eye sockets. In front of us, I noticed that the shute had a ridge of stone in the middle, making it more like two shutes side by side. While I waited for the rush, I speculated which route the boat would take.

Not a speck of water came, and we just sat there. After a while, the Coyotes decided what a good idea it would be to tickle the nasal passage of the elephant with the Yellow Coyote's tail. This would make it sneeze and this would blow us out of the nose. I disagreed: "No! Don't do that because if you get up you will destroy the boat and then we will get separated in the downward blast and maybe we won't find each other again."

But it was too late; they both got out and dis-formed the boat. The yellow one took hold of his own tail and tickled the upper nose of the stone elephant. We were shot forward by a great rush of air and water mixed and we plopped into a pool. I was very pleased to find that they were still with me, but, instead of landing in the beautiful nature pool, we were sitting in the grey, muddy water of a shallow circular depression. All the land around this waterhole was the same mud-grey colour. At a little distance, the surface was rough, dry, and cracked, but it was smooth and slippery around the edges of the pool where the water had splashed onto it. I was deeply disappointed. I thought: "This is hideous."

In an upbeat way, the Coyote asked me: "What do you think of the colour grey?" Even though I was aware that I have started to come to terms with it recently in the attentive form of the grey horse of the Grandfather, I replied mournfully: "I have always hated the colour grey. Everything is the same." He said: "No, everything isn't the same. Everything is grey, but everything isn't the same. Feel the water." I did, and yes, the water was fluid and I absorbed all the feelings of the water. He said: "Now climb out of the pool and feel the ground." Yes, it did feel very different. He was right: the fact that they were all grey had nothing to do with same-ness.

Towards the end of this seminar week there was a total eclipse of the moon which was to happen around three thirty in the morning. Two of us decided to get up to see it. At two fifty I woke and looked out of the window; it was a beautiful clear night and the eclipse was starting. I woke my friend. We rushed a cup of tea and went out to the beach. The full moon light was intense, as we walked, we could see each other clearly and every detail of our shadows moving along the ground. In the final darkening we stood together. A lone goose flew past, honking quietly. Smoky colours of reddish gold and black smudged the surface of the darkened moon and the bright light was utterly gone. We marvelled: "How reflective the moon is, like a mirror." For a long time, we waited and then, still in complete darkness, we walked back, we had no shadows now.

My meditation began with the appearance of a snake, a big brown-coloured snake, like the python from Uluru, coming horizontally from the right and entering my navel centre. Slithering up to my solar plexus, the snake became grey. It filled the entire solar plexus and I found this very strange; I couldn't imagine a grey solar plexus. Then pale-yellow came and I realized the presence of the Grandfather. When the colour red came, I began to see the Grandfather: "Grandfather, Grandfather!"

He came towards me, lifted me up and placed me in his heart centre. That was a deep feeling of love, connection and placement. I had a tiny thought: "Do I deserve it?" and I heard him tell me that I had done well and that everything was right. I began to see the old red-painted wooden house that I had spotted in a local estate agent's window and viewed on a free afternoon during the seminar week. I think I might buy it as a second home to be more often close to my Teacher in Scotland so that I can help to build a Sound Peace Chamber at his place. A Sound Peace Chamber, a space dedicated to exploring the mysteries of sound, a building where people work together awakening personal awareness and seeking the way to world peace.

I left my conscious mind and moved into an appreciation of the incoming flow of the Power, not a flow of personal power which increases my sense of self, but the Power that generates the heartbeat of the Universe. In order to allow the Power to enter I surrendered my understanding, which is a fundamental mechanism of my daily life consciousness, and so I returned, on this occasion, not holding on to what I had experienced. Yes, I think I got the main points down. The old wooden house is good; it is constructed in such a way that the surrounding place can enter in.

A traumatic time yesterday as my enthusiasm and freedom were destroyed by returning to my situation in England and seeing the pain that my partner suffered when I told him I might bid for the wooden house. He immediately allowed no options and said that was the end and everything was to finish between us. The situation is not as straightforward as it seems from what I just described. It would be a long story to tell, but our paths have diverged. Sufficient to say that while we care for each other and our lives have long been intertwined, I have an imperative spiritual call and he has another woman.

This morning, as is my daily practice, I meditated. I went to the Ancient Grandfather, stood beside him and became the quiet attentive calmness of the grey horse. From everything being grey, including the solar plexus, the colour yellow came into my navel centre. Then the colour red came with great power and energy and covered me. It was a very strengthening time.

When my concentration became aware again, I saw a green snake materializing in the darkness and travelling downwards. This snake coiled and coiled and coiled and formed a vortex which led down like a whirlpool, down, down, down, into my solar plexus. I began to travel down the coils of this green snake, which were very fat and substantial as I entered the vortex but became thinner and thinner, the deeper I descended. Eventually I reached the head which was tiny, the size of a thimble. I took the head between the finger and thumb of my right-hand and I pulled it upwards with a tiny pop. There was a minute hole through which I passed. I came into a square black chamber which was the secret egg-chamber of the snake.

There were many white eggs there, and I focused on one. I passed through the wall of this egg and became the embryo inside. I wondered if I would hatch into a snake, and, as I thought about the very great differences between the consciousness of myself and the snake Being, I seemed to expand rapidly until I was an enormously aware Being that looked down, down, down, down into the depths where the tiny egg lay in the chamber. I asked myself when and how I would ever break out of that place. It seemed to me that the place was Life. Yes, life was existence within the white egg of the green snake which lay coiled in an inverted cone within the solar plexus.

I did not know how I would be able to come out of the egg, so I called to the Ancient Grandfather. Seeing him, sitting astride his horse, I walked towards him and, facing him this time, I laid my forehead on his left thigh and I put my left arm up over the neck of the horse and round the waist of the Grandfather so that it touched the part of his back where the right kidney would be and he communicated to me: "Jump on the horse." I jumped up behind him and I put my front, all my open centres, against his spinal column, and there I found my Teacher, and there, golden light was made.

Yes, during this journey I had to fight to maintain the deep concentration needed to stay on it. It made me feel very ill, but, comfortable as my daily life could be it is too boring for me. Last night I sat for a few hours with my partner in front of a nice warm fire watching stuff that I wasn't interested in on the TV. And, while I managed to do this and take the good parts of it as a bonus, I would have much preferred to have been doing something else, even if it involved suffering. So when I was in this journey and it was hurting, or I got exhausted, or I thought I would lose the memory of it, even when I was thinking I was at the limits, I just determined to push on, because otherwise I might as well die. I might as well die, I will never hatch. I will be an addled egg.

## Knowing the Ropes

This morning the Grandfather was here immediately; he came as pale golden light in my lower centres. This light moved up to my heart centre and it shone like a pale watery sun in my heart. I felt it deeply, steadily, shining there. Then the power of the Grandfather moved down to my solar plexus where the colour grey was evident, the colour grey which obscured, or took away, the differences between things, and I thought how this image was like the sun hidden behind grey clouds on a misty day. I stood there, grey in the grey, without any feeling now about this colour except that it must be travelled through to open perception.

Eventually I came back, and I found that my body was no longer an enemy of my spiritual life but that it longed for spirit to be manifested. I saw the old wooden house, which has gone to a sealed bid and I feel I have little chance of ever owning, but I saw a bright orange fire burning in the fireplace in the sitting room. I saw that all the horrible furniture had been cleared out, the house was empty, and it was a very possible house. Yes, that terribly run-down property is a major metaphor of myself.

I saw the white horse ahead of me and today I really loved this horse. Happy to see it, I ran towards it, I put my arms around its neck, hugged it, and said encouragingly: "Eat the grass." But the horse seemed to find this funny and, shaking its mane, it lay down, rolled onto its back and kicked its legs in the air causing grass seeds to fly everywhere. The horse stood up, shook itself free of dust and grey enveloped everything.

When the dust settled, I found myself surrounded by Elders, with the joy of recognition, I exclaimed: "Fathers! Mothers!" There were many of them, and in among them was the Ancient Grandfather. He came forward and he, in front of this Council, acknowledged me and took me as his own. Standing next to him I began to see; I saw a golden X-shape, in which one line was curved and one line was straight.

*bow*

I considered what it could be, and I thought: "It must be a bow and arrow." But I didn't particularly want to see a bow and arrow, wasn't the time of the bow over? The word 'bow' changed into the word 'bow-l', and I saw a golden bowl there, a golden bowl that was a gift for me. I picked it up; it was like half of the golden sphere.

*bow-l*

Inside the bowl I saw round discs like golden coins; I thought with surprise: "Money! money? Spirit money? How very strange to have money here." But the word 'money' was changed to 'treasure'. I noticed: "These golden discs will fit in the energy centres, they are like food." I picked them up one at a time. The first one I put into my throat centre and I felt it being absorbed by my body. The second one I put in my heart. The third one I put into my solar plexus. In each place, although the golden discs were all the same, I felt their different effects on the energy centres, strengthening their individual qualities. I put the next one in the root centre, the next in the eye centre, and the sixth, the last, in the navel centre. In this way treasured by the Ancestors, I returned.

When the Grandfather had acknowledged me in the Council I saw all his yellow bones again and I said something to the assembly which, even at the time, I felt I did not want to record because it was a secret, like a secret earth ceremony, and, funnily enough, now I have completely forgotten what I said, but it was a vow of some kind. It seems to me that it might have given him exclusive rights. I am not sure, to my everyday mind that sounds amusing now, no wonder I did not want to bring the memory back.

Yes, I am unable to gain access to the vow I made to the Grandfather in front of the Elders and I just have to hope that I can keep it without remembering it. I think it is something appropriate to be known in that place only, and all that I can think of now are strange legal terms to do with buying houses, like: 'vacant possession', 'becoming the key holder', phrases like that. Another level of the metaphor of the red house reveals itself.

My meditation began this morning with an overwhelming presence of the sweet, gentle side of my partner. I didn't want it. I didn't want to become ensnared in it because I knew that there was a trap of suffering there, and it couldn't be any other way. I passed through this 'atmosphere'.

The Buffalo appeared and, praying to the Fathers, the Mothers, and the Children, I entered the buffalo skin lodge, a familiar place that I have been to before, but not in this story. In the lodge I felt sure I could get to the Grandfather. I moved through my body in my open-eyed awareness, looking, looking, looking for the Grandfather. I sensed his horse ahead of me. I went up to the horse and I put my hand on its left flank. I jumped up onto the back of the horse behind the Grandfather and laid my body against his spine.

An Eagle appeared, and with the Eagle came the red house. I am regretting not offering more for this building as I have been outbid. The Eagle rolled up the image of the old wooden house into a little red ball and placed it in the left-hand side of my body, just above the hip joint, where it became no more than a flake of red paint from its own exterior wall. The Eagle said: "Scrape that flake of paint away." And the paint scraping fell. I was crying: "No, no," as I watched it fall farther and farther away into the darkness of the void of the limitless ocean. The flake of paint fell down, down, down through the stellar waters and landed on the bottom with all the other debris.

The image of the Grandfather came to me with the words: 'vacant possession' and he entered. I asked myself a few emergency questions about what was going on. Oh well, let it be called: 'vacant possession', that's fine by me, I am just a wrecked old building. Then the Coyote came along, closed my energy centres, brought me back, and dropped me solidly into this world where I am now.

Yesterday was Thursday, so time in the world is still running according to the master plan. I sang and played the drum late into the night. My partner had gone out to the pub. I was happy to be alone. I am finding being in his company pretty hard; I am finding him volatile, unpredictable, threatening to be difficult and then, suddenly, concerned and caring.

Before I began the meditation this morning my navel centre was aching, aching, aching. I have really come to the firm conclusion now that the pain is caused by my resistance. As I lay here I saw the word 'fear' appear in the pain like a living being. I mean that the word had a form and an energy which could be clearly seen. I will try to describe it: the 'F-ii' part was shaped like a V with smooth sides, and the end of the world, I mean, the end of the word, trailed away into nothingness....... nothing, it dissipated everything. So I lay with the intent to release the pain and that is what I did. My navel centre relaxed more and more, and slowly opened. Colours came in extreme intensity. The Power was there. I concentrated on the Power. It was a feeling which moved through my bodies and made them aware.

The Power moved for a long time, whatever a long time is in the meditative state. At times unpleasant things, particularly emotional things, would appear. Like an unpleasant situation with a customer from years ago would suddenly strike me and cause a disruption in my connection to the beautiful stream. I knew these things, however old, had to be resolved, re-solved, because they damage my ability to surrender to the movement of the spirit power.

Last night I had thought on what the Ancient Grandfather said about learning to love what you hate, a teaching which causes me to burst out crying every time I contemplate it. I thought: "How can I love a person who has mean and selfish intent?" I discovered that it is possible to recognize bad intent and still feel love for the person who is suffering from it.

The Grandfather came, transforming everything to the colour grey. I went towards him and entered into the horse. I thought a great deal about the nature of the horse, how I am at ease to be the grey horse connected to the Grandfather, but it is not at all easy for me to ride my white horse. In the grey horse, I enjoyed peace, where no negative thoughts were evident, till the Coyotes, yellow and black, came and stood on either side of my brain where I was grey in the middle (the phrase 'grey matter' comes to mind now), they brought me back here. I thank everybody and everything that helped me to explore the aspects of being and doing that I have explored today.

I discovered the Yellow Coyote on his own and in a new and close-to-me furry animal-form. I passed through him into the presence of the Grandfather and I walked down the left-hand side of the horse's body and round behind the tail. I, in my everyday world self, did not want to stand behind the tail of the horse and understand the enormous energy of that region, so I passed quickly by, but I overcame my reluctance and returned to observe the powerful haunches and to touch the long, glossy tail.

My solar plexus opened as I stood there, and, having absorbed that tremendous energy, I moved to the right side of the horse. I noticed that it was a roan; its rump speckled with darker grey spots against a lighter grey background. I saw a hand print there, a red hand, this filled me with pleasure. I looked again, and the hand print was blue. I looked for a third time, and the hand print was yellow. I took a step along the side of the horse and I thought: "The Grandfather's lance should be here." It was. The point was shaped like a spearhead with a ball behind it, and the head, made of silver, was divided down its length between black and white. Shattering power, in the sense of breaking up my preconceptions, came into the centre of me and very swiftly I passed into the energy of the solar plexus.

I became aware of a fish-like Being that was curled up there, tightly curled into a ball. My solar plexus was enormous and still this fish filled it. I released the tension and the fish uncoiled, it was a Whale Shark, the largest fish of all, and, once it was released, it began to swim away into the dark oceanic void. The creature that was left, which was me, was a pilot fish. The pilot fish wanted to swim with the whale shark, but I did not want to disappear with the whale shark, away from some shell which was my consciousness that I wished to remain in contact with. I did a curious thing, I decided the pilot fish was my ego and I let it go while I remained behind. I watched the whale shark until it disappeared.

I, in the sense of my I-less-ness, remained behind, and when I looked at myself, I saw just a curl of smoke rising. The curl of smoke was rising from round the edges of a silver surface that was like a mirror. The ever-curious Black Coyote appeared, and we went to inspect this silvered surface. It was a fluid, like mercury, and it filled a white bowl, like the crucibles we used in the chemistry laboratories at school. The Coyote tipped the crucible over with his nose because he knew that worms and things like that often hid beneath bowls and he was hungry. There were earthworms underneath and he sucked them up like spaghetti. There were a few centipedes, grey woodlice, creatures like that, and I think we ate the lot.

I went from the turning over of the bowl into an extended journey into the colour grey, finding the colour grey an amazing place to wander in. I imagined that I would not leave the grey. I would stay there. It was a place of great simplicity. In the mist there was enough light to make me feel connected, without the necessity to struggle for images. I wandered for a long time in the grey light, suddenly feeling that I liked it, grateful to the Grandfather for showing me this light.

Last night there was a programme on TV called *Stone Age Man*. There was opening footage of the Bushmen in Africa and, to my complete surprise, it was a programme about shamanic practices. There was an ancient rock painting from the Drakensfeld where the person who had taken on the power of the Eland was holding its tail: in my journey yesterday, I had experienced the power of the grey horse in a similar way. There was another correspondence when Bushmen of the present day talked about the body pain experienced by a medicine person: the pain was associated with the presence of the Power. The picture of a person all broken up without a head was a person praying to the Power. Yes, this was all very stunning to me. I kept very quiet and didn't respond to any of my partner's remarks and enquiries. I sat there absorbed, grateful to see how old the things are which have come to me.

During tea time today, I initiated a discussion with my partner about whether to change the date of closing the business that we run together and bring it forwards by three months. This was a rational discussion, but later it prompted an emotionally difficult conversation where he expressed his anger that, what he considered to be, 'mumbo jumbo' was causing the break-up of our life together. I tried to explain to him that we have grown apart, but I didn't mention the fact that I know about his girlfriend. I thought afterwards how unhappy this conversation made me, but how silly I am to consider myself responsible for his wellbeing when he is perfectly capable of looking after himself.

Late at night I played the drum and, before I started, I said: "This is for the Grandfathers." I played. I sang to the Ancient Grandfather. When I opened my eyes, I expected to see him because he was so present.

I woke this morning. Remembering that it is leap year day, I lay here and opened myself up, got rid of my thoughts, and waited. Awareness and Placement, '-ii' and '-eh', began to play together as contiguous quarters of the medicine wheel, West and South. Their colours, black and white, mixed together and they made the colour grey. I had found myself in the greyness.

A thick and densely woven rope, like a hawser from a ship, so heavy that it hung in a completely straight line, was before me. It reminded me of the trunk of a palm tree, but it was not a tree, it was a rope. I looked up and I couldn't see where it came from. I looked down and I couldn't see where it was going to: "That is gravity at work. Shall I go up, or shall I go down? I will go straight in. That is the best thing to do."

I travelled forward into the brown rope. The woven strands were like a spiral staircase and I began, even against my inclination, to go down the spiral. As I descended, I met another Being also descending. It was a nature Being of some sort, like the one that the Grandfather pulled out of the ground that time. I suggested: "Shall we travel together?" But this proved to be quite hard for me, I kept losing my ability to perceive that Being and, when that happened, I had to search and find it again. Eventually we came to the bottom of the rope.

Now I could look intently at my travelling companion; it began to shrink. I bent over it and watched it diminish until it became a tiny little speck. I began to decrease my size in order to maintain my perception of it, but it became so small that it was indistinguishable from the ground. Suddenly it popped up behind me the same size as myself. I spun round, full of admiration, exclaiming: "Wow, that was a neat trick!"

It was a Being like myself and we began to twist together like two strands of a spiral. We twisted, and, as we twisted, we rose. We rose and rose and rose to a golden place where I saw the Grandfather who was golden-yellow, exactly the same colour as the place he was in, and even the horse was yellow. I went towards them thinking, with joy: "In this place I can look steadfastly at the Grandfather. In this place I can do anything I want." So, standing behind him on his right-hand side, I leapt onto the horse and right into him. Then I knew I would be able to look out of his eyes and that was a moment of trauma, a moment of: "What does the Grandfather see?"

I looked out of his eyes, and I saw that we were high up on an escarpment, below us a grey featureless plain stretched away. On the plain, at a far distance, there was something struggling, something trying to walk. I zoomed in on it and saw a solitary jet black buffalo trying to get to its feet, staggering, unable to stand, falling; watching its struggle was awful. I embraced it with my solar plexus and, when it was encompassed, I made the colour green and wrapped the black buffalo in the green. I found myself to be looking down at the Earth. The planet was the Buffalo with the greenness on its surface. The solar plexus was all the layers of the atmosphere, the envelope which is an integral part of the Earth. Outside of this there was a golden Me-ness observing it, trying to do something to diminish the not-ness of the Black Buffalo.

Unaccountably I began to drift, to drift in the golden world. Nothing felt wrong about this; I just became completely detached and, out of my own control, drifted. In time the Coyotes arrived; they made a ball enfolding me within. This ball was heavy enough to come to a halt, something I could not do because, as the drifting Being, I had no mass and no momentum of my own.

We were still, but I was nowhere near my normal consciousness and I wondered how I would get back. Nothing seemed to move. I understood that I should put myself entirely in the hands of the Grandfather and that he would move me. It required a moment of great willingness to allow this to happen and I managed to change my mental attitude to accommodate this request. I waited, and it was reasonably nice to wait, to allow, to surrender. I felt the intense prickliness of the Grandfather come, and I felt myself go into some further state of unconsciousness.

Then, after ........., well, the next thing I knew was that I was moving, and the Grandfather moved me back through the journey, through, through, through. I don't know where I went, but anyway here I am, and that will probably do.

Yes, as I came out, I saw a section of the story Joseph tells where his Grandfather comes back from the other world with summer flowers in his hand when it is winter in the place where they are living. This was a metaphor of what the Grandfather is asking of me, which is to bring images from the inner plains back to the world of everyday.

### A Modern Jumble

I travelled extensively through very strange spaces which contained modern imagery. I could not make a coherent story out of them, but I allowed myself to be taken further and further, observing these images as they passed. I spent an extended time with Joseph in the colour purple. He put a purple square, somewhat like a television screen, into my forehead and I concentrated on that. Eventually I seemed to end up with the Grandfather, and the last image I saw was of a mirror being polished with a yellow duster. That is what the meditation was like. I felt extremely altered at the end of it and it has taken me some time to recover. I feel there is a message in this confusing jumble of images from the modern world which is that I do not know how to make sense of my own experience and this life.

A day or two has passed. I didn't record my meditation yesterday; it was too much for me. I went through so many barriers and changed shape so many times that I couldn't deal with it and I didn't put any of the images down on tape. I remember now an image of a white ice sheet forming over a tipi and myself going into the tipi. I remember going somewhere with the Grandfather that was a great change of state, a great gate to pass through.

Yesterday was also a hard day in the world of everyday. I have spent three days working with my partner again and feel myself to be in a fairly shattered state. I feel that he is making a massive effort, somewhere that is not here, to detach me from my spirit life. Of course, I am fighting this interpretation, saying: "It is within me that this conflict is generated."

So, I didn't feel the least bit connected to the spiritual this morning. No, I was too preoccupied with all these difficulties and the fact that, even though it is Saturday, I feel I should work today because I am going away for a week and the paperwork and organisation of the business is getting too chaotic and needs serious sorting.

I was thinking about all these conflicting stresses, but as soon as I crossed the mental barrier into an altered state it was very different, very beautiful. But the beautiful side of my partner was there too! My impulse would have been to tell it to go away, but instead I allowed myself to stay still and observe this beautiful part.

Then a point in my body drew my attention, and I homed in on this point within the great body of my awareness and travelled there. I began to learn; that is when the colour grey came, and I found myself without preliminaries in the grey horse, I thought: "I just entered the horse of the Grandfather without any appreciation of him, or the shape of the horse, or any other transition. How did that happen? Just by seeing the colour grey? Still, I know where I am and I will go with this."

I could sense that the Grandfather was riding the horse. The Grandfather pulled the horse's head round to the right and we turned and went into the right. We began to gallop. It made me laugh, it had become very like a child's game of horses. I suddenly remembered how at playtime in infant school we used to play horse and rider. My very good friend was Roy Rogers and I used to play being Trigger, his horse. I was laughing to myself thinking: "Look at how this has come from your deep subconscious to form this experience, and is this all just a joke, or how does it work?"

I decided: "I don't care, because I was utterly miserable and in conflict before I began to meditate this morning but now, I am happy, I am interested, I am stretched in my abilities, and I feel that I am doing the thing that I want to do."

I galloped with the Grandfather through the grey world; we were galloping through mist, we were galloping through cloud, we were galloping through smoke; until we came to a halt in front of an immense reflective disc. There is a place where the reflective surface can be penetrated, and you can go through, but in all the journeys I have taken so far I have not gone through the mirror skin. I knew: "Today I am going through." For a moment, I felt myself pressed up against the silvered surface, while behind us was all the smoke and cloud through which we had travelled, then the Grandfather urged me through.

He was standing beside me now and I said to myself: "Do not allow any of your rational beliefs or anxieties to cloud what you can see." I looked around and I saw light. It was clear light which had the potential of all the seven colours in it, but I knew that the minute I searched for any one of those colours I would begin to lose the appreciation of the non-separateness. So it came to me that when you go through the mirror you go into something which essentially is of no interest. That is partly a joke, but what I mean is that there is no variety there, it is the One Thing. Of course, I was still a conscious Being, still a split-off thing observing the One Thing, and so I didn't completely, perhaps, understand its nature, but I understood something about the One-ness, and how easy it was for me to split it into the many. It was all the consequent diversions and diversity that the splitting of the light brought with it that I was after experiencing.

I sensed that we were going to return, and I maintained my detached no-questioning state and tried to observe the changes as we returned. In fact, what this meant was that the Grandfather came back with me in a different kind of way. I was thinking with him, if you like, in his thoughts, and not struggling to seize the experiences with my interpretative mind. I slowly observed the changes in the greyness which became denser and denser. I also began to feel very, very ill, but I put that on one side, and I came through it all with the Grandfather who returned like grey smoke and, opening my eyes and looking out of the window, I see that somebody has lit a fire in the house across the road and grey smoke is coming out of the chimney and it is reminding me again of the Grandfather.

Some time later there I was again, completely confused and in a mess. Even before I started to meditate my navel centre was so painful, I was, well, almost in despair, and I called out: "Please somebody, something I know, come to me." A very familiar presence came, but I didn't know who or what it was, there was some way in which I was not ready.

I called again, and I entered the spirit lodge of the buffalo. It was asked of me: "Why am I making things so difficult when the deep connection has been established?" "Why am I searching and questioning and making my time difficult?" Well: "Why am I?" Because I encounter a lot of incomprehensible stuff, that's why. But I decided: "Ok, I will accept the incomprehensible as part of it, and I will travel."

The lodge today was completely empty, as if being deliberately kept empty for my sake. I saw the great open space of the internal world of the buffalo. I drifted through that space and I realized that I must stop living out on the right-hand side of my awareness and move to the centre. Overcompensating, I moved far to the left-hand side of my awareness, and there I decided I would lie down and rest. The minute I rested everything went grey and the image of an elephant began to form. I was confused because the grey elephant was the place of stuck-ness in the drum journey, but grey is also the teaching colour of the Grandfather. I decided: "I will accept this confusion."

I found myself immersed in the pool into which we dropped on that drum journey. This time I thought: "I rather like this pool. It is sensual, the sides are smooth, the mud is slippery and shiny, the water is lukewarm and shallow, and it is altogether rather pleasant." I realized that I was sitting in my navel centre. The feelings in my navel centre were very delicious. I scooped up the water in my hands and rubbed it round the ring of the mud pool so that it became smoother and smoother. The sensual pleasure of this was delightful and, when the circle was completed, wonderful feelings of warmth and pleasure emanated from the centre. Soft golden light shone, and I did hear a phrase something like 'the enjoyment of the golden light'.

Eventually I moved away from there, up, up, up. It became painful again and I asked myself: "Why? Why did I find it necessary to move?" But I did. I came back to the great circular space of the buffalo spirit lodge. I saw I was in the very centre of this space. I felt a bit too important stood at the centre of the whole thing there. I allowed myself, for a millisecond, to feel myself to be the centre of everything. Then I let the picture go.

## The Peace Tree

I woke up this morning dreaming of Joseph. He was directing a ceremony. He called out: "Let the meditators collect here and do their job. Then the rest of you come and we will do the ceremony." I was so eager: I knew I was one of the meditators. I looked up from where I was, looked into his eyes and went towards the place he had indicated for us to gather. When I woke up a huge feeling of love and intent was with me. How typical of Joseph was the way he was teaching, without compulsion and without rigidity, only with suggestion, waiting for us to pull out of our Beings the inspiration that we needed to perform that ceremony.

I began to meditate, and at the moment my mind is a blank, so I must just go and think. ........ I think I will have to say it started with that deep feeling of love entering my perception at the level of my navel, and I went with this feeling utterly and without reservation. I went also without thoughts, without preconceptions, without putting any ideas upon the experience; I simply accepted that this was an incomprehensible but beautiful feeling that came from somewhere and all I needed to do was connect to it and accept it.

Golden light began to be apparent. In the ancient light the Grandfather was visible. Then a she-Bear appeared, lying on her belly, and the Grandfather said to me: "You can enter the body of the bear; you know where the entrance is." The entrance was on the left-hand side, between the neck and the shoulder. I went in. The inside was like a great cathedral and I lay down flat on the ground with my belly against the bear's belly. At the far end of the bear was some great place of power, and, as I looked at the place of power, I felt my belly splitting open.

I went through the slit and, I believe, it was at that point that I saw a great pine tree ahead of me. This Pine Tree had fallen without breaking and its root entire mass was pulled out of the ground. The base of the tree that was exposed had an entrance that was not a locked door to those who could go in. The trunk was hollow, and I know I went into the tree to wait for more people to come. After a while I looked around, and if the bear was the nave of the cathedral then the pine tree was the steeple. The spirits spoke to me about peace. They showed me my partner and they said: "Peace." They did not say world peace, just peace. Peace must exist now within your own place, within your own heart, within your own life, within your close relationships. I really felt that world peace existed in those moments of every individual life and that it wasn't the great concept of struggling to stop all wars. It was the concept of struggling for peace in my own patch, the place where I am standing, my placement.

I was in this state of enraptured ecstasy within the peace tree when the most enormous full moon began to rise. I was taken to the face of the moon. My body and face were scrubbed upon its surface like I was being washed by a cleansing sponge, during that process I returned here.

I had a contest with my partner at tea time yesterday where he tried to have a go again at undermining my spiritual life. He accused me of running away from his questions and fudging the issue. They are not questions at all really, but attacks in a battle. I told him that I knew he would never give up trying to attain his goal of proving there is no spirit, and that I did not want to go to the final wall with him for the final battle. I didn't tell him that I thought there would be two dead bodies there, but I asked him to accept that he didn't know when to give up. This giving up that I was talking about was not surrender; it was about giving up the overriding need to attain the objective. He replied that is what he had been trained for in the armed forces and he accepted my point of view.

I have been travelling, meditating, relaxing, and being healed since about seven this Sunday morning and it is now ten to eleven, so certain aspects may be forgotten. For example, I don't remember the beginning of my meditation, but eventually the Grandfather of the greyness came to fetch me. He lifted me onto the back of his horse, and when he too was astride the horse, I put my energy centres against his. The horse shifted on its back legs as if getting ready to move and I felt ill. Then the Grandfather encouraged the horse to gallop, and it did gallop. Then it broke into a cantering gait and, oh, I felt bad, I whispered to the Grandfather: "I feel ill with the movement." He replied: "You are too exhausted."

Spirits, many spirits, came and lifted me off the back of the horse. They carried me a little way and dug a pit in the ground. They placed me in the pit and covered me over except for my nose.

Then they scraped away the earth over my navel centre, and my navel centre was energized with the colour blue from the sky while my body was lying in the dark body of Mother Earth, being healed.

Then they took away the earth from the solar plexus. The colour green was growing there, that thin layer of green between the brown earth and the blue sky. I saw the three colours: blue, green, and brown. I saw the dynamic and magical exchanges of energy that take place between them.

They took away the earth from my heart centre. My heart centre was a pool of water. As I looked at this pool the colours of the medicine wheel were evident to me; yellow on my right, black on my left, white above my head and red at my feet; from these four directions came four horses. They walked towards the pool and, when they reached the water, they drank from the pool of my heart centre. The image filled me with love. Suddenly they raised their heads and began to mill about. They were very nervous, they panicked, and they ran towards my lower centres.

A mountain lion had come and was lapping at the water of the pool. It looked up and said to me: "It is easy to remember what you have lost." It meant this: "It is easy to remember all your past lives and right back to the beginning, recalling everything you need to know" but it was said in a very simple sentence: "It is easy to remember what you have lost." The double meaning strikes me now, and I think: "Try to remember what you have found, not dwell on what you have lost."

In the afternoon I sorted out the wood pile and I hurt my back while doing it. I was angry that my partner had not packed the wood properly in the first place, and, in a fit of pique, I ignored the pain for twenty-four hours. When I came to bed last night, I was horrified to discover that I couldn't lie flat. I was in agony and I thought how stupid I was to have let it happen. I had to sleep most of the night on my back, luckily it eased, and I had a reasonably good sleep. Today it was not so bad as long as I kept moving but when I lay down the pain was again astronomical. I have to blame myself; my anger only turned around and hurt me. I have been making a few mistakes lately, and often, when I come to meditate,

I drift into dreams about where I am going to live. I realize that it is very important to me to have a secure base. At the end of the day I created music for the spirits, but I didn't ask them to cure me because I knew it was completely my own fault and I should take the consequences of it.

Last night I also typed up the meditation where I went to the Council of Elders. This morning, immediately I began to meditate, I could see the place where they were. I thanked the spirits for the inspiration which they gave me when I started this travelling practice, to record on tape the experiences at an intermediate state of consciousness between out there and the world of everyday, because this means that, although I carry scant memory of these experiences, when I hear my taped description they come back to me in detail. Without the inspiration to record them, I would have lost them for ever.

The Ancient Grandfather came. It was so easy to walk to him and jump onto his horse. It is only two days since I hurt my back, but, in the travelling world, I was so light, so happy, so full of energy. Sitting behind the Grandfather I noticed that the front of the horse was painted red and the haunches, where I was sitting, were painted yellow, but I knew that underneath the paint his horse was grey, and that made a triangle of the three colours of the Grandfather: grey and yellow and red. This was completely in order; the Grandfather is a triangle of power made from the South West, the North, and the East, and he sits on his horse exactly in the North East.

*the Grandfather's colours*

He sent me travelling through some colours and states that were threatening to me and unpleasantly painful. I heard the echo of his voice following me, saying: "This is why you need to be connected in love or you could never get through these places." I came through those places into a world of pink light. It was like the Great Plain, but it was entirely composed of quartz crystal of the most beautiful shade of pink.

I looked at the shapes and forms that existed there, and I walked in that place. They asked me what I wanted, and I said: "I came to understand. I want to understand all the incomprehensible things that I encounter and be able to know them in my conscious life."

In front of me on the crystal plain they placed a pure crystal Coyote sat on its haunches, looking so perky and so pure and so delightful. I enfolded my body around it and sucked it in through my belly. I myself, I noticed, seemed also to be made of pink quartz. The Coyote and I were utterly one.

Then they gave me the most beautiful pearl that was opalescent and fabulously creamy-silver coloured. I put that in my centre of seeing and everything became so clear. I saw nothing but the rosy crystalline world, yet I felt as if I had total vision. I saw a set of double-sided steps, there were three steps on either side and on the top of these steps the pearl was placed. As I looked, I saw it in three forms, as a pearl, as a bowl, and as a sickle, and it struck me most forcibly that it was the moon.

*the steps of the moon*

I knew I was beginning to return from the crystal plain because the sensation of the Grandfather came back to me. I stretched my spine, and something went click very loudly up between my shoulder blades. The Grandfather laid his right-hand in front of me; it was only composed of bones. I began to touch these disarticulated bones and, as I touched them, they became a living hand again. They became a great hand which took hold of me; the middle finger ran up my body from my heart right up to my head centre; the two fingers on either side curled over and placed themselves on my shoulders, beside the neck where the muscle bunches are, the fingertips touching the place where it feels as if there are holes that go right down into the chest; the little finger and thumb curled round my body, the thumb touched the place on my back which had clicked and the little finger touched higher up, then they moved down and placed themselves firmly over my kidneys. The palm of this great hand connected to my solar plexus and through it came a great yellow-coloured power. That was a most interesting experience which led me into total contact with the Grandfather.

I came back, and back, and laid for a long time in the presence of the Grandfather, just feeling grateful that the spirits stood by me while I suffered from terrible anger. Through that anger I maintained my patience, knowing that it would be temporary, knowing that I hurt myself needlessly, and, determining never to feed it again, I let it run its course.

## Dancing the Grandfather

I will just think for a moment about the recent Sun Moon Dance, the second one to be danced in the UK. Let me see, yes, I was dancing there, and I felt very happy, even when I was feeling headachy and sick on the second day, I felt happy. The spirits were smiling, and I felt that they viewed all our suffering with compassionate amusement. It may sound strange, but at the time I just felt this about my suffering: "It is not that very, very important really" and I laughed about it.

On the third day the Ancient Grandfather came to me as I danced. He asked me to dance to the Tree for him to exercise his legs. As I did this I was taken through his agony of body and spirit as he sacrificed himself in the ceremony and after this time, which was very sad for me, he asked me to change my dress to the snake dress. I had looked at this hand-dyed, hand-painted dress, which I had bought at Uluru and had with me in the arbour, the day before and had decided that I was not going to wear it, but he asked me to put it on, and he told me that I would be called to the Tree in the next dance, and so it happened.

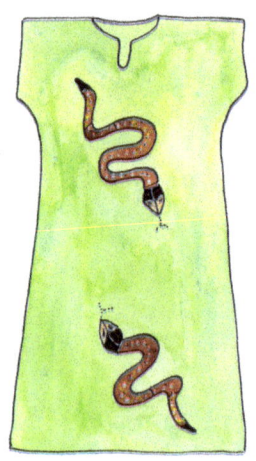

*a dance dress*

I knew when it was time because a great grey cloud formed itself above the top of the Tree and that was the signal for me to go to the Grandfather. Later in the day, when I was dancing again, the Grandfather would say to me: "Just take a stroll." As I went towards the Tree, I would hear this: "Taking a stroll, to the pole, with the Grandfather." It was light, like that.

Some people see the spirit world separate to, but moving in, the physical world. I mean that they see spirits in spirit bodies walking in this world, but I don't seem to have the talent for that. I see the spirit world infusing the forms of the physical world, or else I see the spirit world when I am travelling. In travelling, sometimes it appears as I suspect it really is, and that is incomprehensible to me; other times it appears in metaphors of things that exist in this world so that I can understand it. But I wonder if I will ever see the spirits in this world with my eyes open? Maybe it takes another few years of work.

### The Circle of Awareness

Well, I am not sure about putting this on the tape at all, but I will press on. I came to meditate and found myself disturbed by this life, wanting to be back in the dance arbour, difficult as that is at times, because a great wall of protection is there which helps to concentrate my mind. Laying my distress down, I opened my awareness and the Grandfather was there. I saw the Tree and I saw the exact point on the left-hand side, high up so I had to jump for it, the point that the Grandfather had shown me I should touch when I ran to the pole. I touched it again now in my meditation and I went through into the presence of the Grandfather behind the Tree, through into that other world.

The Grandfather was present in three circles of energy; grey and yellow and red, and, when the red was in the middle with grey above and yellow below, the red ball of energy burst its banks and flooded everything. I felt it in my body colouring every part with red, and all of me became red. I stayed in this red energy for a long time.

Suddenly my mind began to wander; I wanted to get up and have an incredibly practical day. I was saying to myself: "Yes, yes, this is a practical day. Stop meditating now, get up and get things done." But when I examined my state, I discovered that the energy was gripping me hard and I felt that maybe I was trying to run away from something. The Grandfather said to me: "Don't freak out. No matter what happens, go forward." I made a determined effort to change my state of consciousness and I went forward.

Before this I had been seeing some black points of light, and I think that is what set me off wanting to go and do the shopping. So now I concentrated, and I went into the blackness. It became more and more all-embracing, and more and more smooth. I found myself lying face down in a dark world, my mouth against the darkness of a dark pool whose surface was in my navel centre and its depths in my root centre.

Lying there, I became aware of a Black Panther. It put its front paws upon me, and began to work on my lower back, opening up my body and adjusting the bones of my spine in the pelvic region, finding there two downwards pointing spikes on the pelvic girdle. These were black spines with red tips, as if they were hollow and had a fire inside. They were pushed into contact with the ground while my face remained touching the waters of the black pool.

I thought to myself: "The Grandfather was right, do not freak out at anything that happens, because this is so weird, I can't imagine what is going on." I became aware of a strange, fleshy, semi-comatose black snake-like creature. I seemed to flatten it out and push it with my spine against the walls of a great curved shell and, in this way, I took it into my body where something happened to it and I lost my horror of it. But I have to say that I do not understand what was happening there.

My solar plexus became a circle of dark ground. Suddenly the left foot of the Grandfather with his soft moccasin upon it trod into this area, clear as day. I looked at where the big toe of the moccasin touched the ground and growing there was the tiniest green plant. I spoke with excitement: "Oh look Grandfather, a tiny green shoot!" It bore two leaves, like two little tongues coming out of the earth together, bulbous, full of water, and bright green against the darkness of the earth. Busy observing it, I shrank until I was so small that the side of the shoot was like the side of a great ship and I could slip between that and the earth and feel the smooth greenness growing there, making my body feel good.

I came back, and in the conscious state I let my solar plexus feel these things, and I let the energy I had experienced in the altered state charge up my body like a battery and move into my conscious world. Thank you, Grandfather, for that. At the end I stood by the Grandfather, leaning against his horse. Its coat was no longer only grey, it had a rose-pink tinge, like the pink on the grey of a wood pigeon's plumage. The horse was exquisitely beautiful and quietly powerful.

I woke up this morning very disturbed, very overcome by the difficulties emanating from the break up between my partner and I. As I lay here, horribly enmeshed in this agony, and attempted to meditate everything went black and, in the blackness, I saw Joseph. I began to call his name and I was surprised how easily the horrible confusion and battering I was getting disappeared and a space was created in which I stood within Joseph's dark calmness. Purple light came after a while, green also, and I clearly saw the Sun Moon Dance Chief in the purple and green poncho that he wore at the recent UK Dance. I saw the purple and green medicine bundle that was placed under the Tree.

Then, in the midst of the purple and green, I saw a round column, cut off at the top and the bottom, and covered in small yellow and black checks. What a peculiar visual image it was, a column of yellow and black checks the size of the tiny squares of a mosaic, suspended in the world of black and purple and green. I thought what a garish combination of colours it would be in the world of everyday but, there was no doubt, they were all arranged together there in the other world.

I went towards that column and laid the front of my body upon it, feeling the energy. Then I focused intensely on one yellow square. I felt the immense power of the tiny square and out of that small square I pulled all the power that was there. Then I switched my attention to a black square, I felt and did the same with that. The feeling of the two energies was different. The energy of the yellow square was smooth and enlightening and nourishing to the higher centres and the energy was warm. The energy of the black square was emptier, clearer, contained more space, and it energised the lower centres, opening the vast worlds of travelling that exist there. Both squares led to greater awareness, but the yellow was a condensed awareness whereas the black was a diffused awareness. How generous the Coyotes are!

I looked again at a yellow square, again at a black square, and they began to merge together. I fought to avoid this amalgamation, but the Coyote said to me: "No, it is an eclipse." I saw the smoky mixture of these colours on the face of the eclipsed moon, and I realized I was going through a barrier. As I went through everything became grey and I became aware of the Grandfather. I passed through the greyness, moving towards the body of the horse; that is where I wanted to be.

As I approached the horse I said: "I don't think I knew your name." And the horse said: "My name is Listener, '-ii-eh-uu', Listener." I went straight into the grey listening space, but no sooner had I felt the Grandfather upon my back than he pulled me out of the body of the horse so that I stood in front of him. I was grey, and he was pale golden-yellow and, holding me to him, he said: "Do not freak out about anything that happens now." I remembered he had said this to me yesterday and at other times and so I was prepared today.

The Grandfather began to send his energy into my awareness.

I felt my navel centre begin to move and the energy came through my back, through my kidneys, and into my navel centre. I saw the green snake coming from the Grandfather and coiling itself up in my body. A blue snake followed it. Then, as I looked at that energy centre, I saw that a black snake and a yellow snake were also there. Four snakes there, moving and coiling and raising their heads in that centre, and I marvelled at the snake power of this Grandfather.

Suddenly I was standing at the opening of my heart centre. I never felt so aware of the great world of the heart into which I could step through a circular opening like entering into another dimension. I stood there for a moment and what did I see? I saw green. I saw vibrant emerald green stretching forever, the grass of the Great Plains. I stepped through onto that grass. Never did I feel so present in my heart centre. Never did I have such a feeling of the complete circle of awareness which is the heart centre.

Standing there I saw, in the far distance, a red Being approaching. I tried to see what it was; I wanted it to be an animal. Was it a buffalo? Was it a deer? But the advice given to me was: "Do not make it anything. Let it come to you and be what it is." When it arrived, it was the shape and colour of a flame, bright red against the bright green, such a strong and opposite colour combination. It didn't flicker like a flame on Earth, but it was a red flame on the grasslands.

"What is this flame?" I asked myself and the Great Voice answered me: "This flame is Life, Life in all its forms." The flame, this is my interpretation, the flame is the ability of Life to transform itself into many, many different animal forms all created and nourished and built from the greenness.

I felt that power of Life. I not only felt the great redness of the spirituality that made the life forms, but I also felt all the apparent horror of the colour red: bleeding, violence, death. Those things were also inherent in this flame and they were all about gaining insights right up against the worst situations. That is how it appears to me now; it wasn't like that there. There it was the red flame of Life burning and moving on the Great Plain.

I have completely lost how I came back, but I think the Grandfather must have transformed me back into my grey self. I think he laid his hands upon my back and, yes, there was a long process of breathing in the Power and letting it out with quiet noise as the air left my lungs.

Last night I was in the middle of sending some e-mails when the electricity began to stutter and fluctuate. The computer froze, so badly that I had to unplug it and leave the battery to run down in order to free it up.

I woke this morning and I travelled for an hour or so through many images with which I am familiar. When, after an hour, I came back and lay on my side, I spirit-dreamed; that is what I call it. I surrender my mind and I am semiconscious. Dreaming, but not deeply unaware, I let the spirits take me to whatever experiences they give me. Today I ended up in my new house in Scotland. I went out into the garden to hang out some washing, but I noticed my body felt very peculiar and I realized I was astral travelling. Could anybody see me? Then I realized I was dreaming, and I became conscious in that dream.

I came back and lay here for a while until I felt the spirits call me and the Grey Grandfather was there. He came, reminding me of the events of the Sun Moon Dance. I welcomed him; I appreciated his presence and spoke my gratitude. A beautiful Rose made of rose quartz crystal appeared in my hands, then it was lifted and taken up onto the crossbeam of a shape made of three beams, two vertical and one horizontal. As the Rose was placed on the flat edge of the horizontal beam I heard: "That is the gift of Love."

I thought: "Yes, and it is up there." Intending to retrieve it, I threw a rope over the beam. But, seeing it hanging there, I knew that if I climbed the rope, I would be hung and that would be how I would obtain the Rose. Did I want to die like that?

Returning, I lay thinking about this experience. As I had briefly held the Rose, the gift of Love, it sparkled in the light and was so crystal clear and beautiful. When it was placed on the crossbeam, I knew that it was safe, and I knew where it was, but I do not understand why it was taken out of my hands.

I began to think intensely about the Grandfather dying on the ceremonial Tree. I asked myself again in what way was this different to Jesus? I felt that sacrifice to be so similar, but the Grandfather came forward and spoke to me. He told me how it was not the same. It was not the same because the people who killed Jesus hated him and wanted to get rid of him, whereas the Grandfather had offered to die and was helped to die by the people who loved him; they were all part of the sacrifice: that was the difference.

It was hard for me to understand what he meant; but, maybe, he meant this: Jesus was executed by his enemies and their negative intention would always remain active alongside the Love he brought to the people. But there was no negative intent in the sacrifice of the Grandfather and therefore love alone came into the world with his sacrifice.

When I drummed tonight the drum was very loud, the beat was very fast, and the experience was very uplifting. I saw something new coming, a female spirit dressed in a grey shift and red was about her upper body and her head. She was related to the Grandfather and I was singing a wild and crazy happy song.

## In Relation To

I woke in the night to the presence of love. The Spirit of Love was here, touching me, and it was beautiful. I woke this morning and that Spirit returned. The golden light of the sunrise was filling the sky and it was beautiful.

I travelled with Love and I was reminded of what I have learnt about why human beings, myself included, are so attracted to negative thinking. It is because the acute sensitivity of feeling that comes with love brings with it all the suffering in the world and it is not possible to be immune to those sufferings. I understand this now.

I kept asking questions and at this stage of a meditation a question destroys utterly, utterly destroys, the connection to the incoming spirit. I managed to move away from the questions and be carried by Love into some very altered states. At one point the power of Love slowly rose up my body, coming to rest in my meditative eye, and I felt my face disappearing. I understood the metaphor of the face, which is a barrier between one thing and another, and my face disappeared. I entered into the spirit that was around me and I travelled.

I saw the Eagle as a great golden sphere, and I knew there were five spheres emanating from that Eagle Being and that they were the vibrations which made the created world. All the five spheres of light were golden-yellow from a distance but as I approached them, they took up their individual colour vibrations. I found myself travelling towards the sphere of the right shoulder of the great bird and I entered the green. The bird folded its wings around all the emanations, which condensed into the centre of its Being into one great ball of vibrating purple light and in that light, there was Joseph. I travelled to the centre and I must have lost it.

When I came to, the Ancient Grandfather was carrying me

out of the centre in his consciousness and I felt this to be so much where I wanted to be that I called out: "I want to be closer, to be more aware of you, Grandfather." I heard the phrase 'in relation to' and I began to be aware of a young Being all made from the yellow light. This young spirit girl moved closer to me and I knew that she was becoming in me. And, of course, so it was, how could there be a grandfather without a grandchild? That is what the phrase 'in relation to' meant, because in the consciousness of separation everything is in relation to everything else.

I was feeling very exhausted by now, and, though I longed to stay out in the travelling state, I think it was becoming too much for my physical body. I felt the Coyotes nearby, black and yellow, they would bring me closer to this world.

Yes, when I was feeling very ill, I thought: "I could be happy living in Scotland doing a bit of gardening, pottering around, getting a part-time job, just being like that." But I knew there was no question of me only doing that. I think what I must do is learn to thoroughly enjoy that world of everyday and learn to wait for the spirits to call me. I don't have to struggle anymore to connect. I have to struggle when I am connected, but I have struggled for so long it is part of my psyche, I just have to change the area of struggle.

### Tree

It was early yesterday evening that suddenly the photograph of Joseph was speaking to me. I felt such a surge of joy when this happened that it made me wish to thank the spirit world for all that my Teachers in human form have done for me, and so I sang, taking the vowel sounds of their names and singing a little, or even, a BIG song in praise of each of their lives.

I came to meditate this morning and I found myself in the

english Sun Moon Dance arbour. I found my body lying across the dance ground, my head in the South and my feet in the North. The the Dance Tree, which was white, was planted in my navel centre. I felt my body moving, changing, my toes and my head stretched upwards, curving to touch the place where the trunk becomes branches.

I looked at the white Tree growing out of my body and I saw all the life-force which I contain being drawn from my body up the trunk as nutrition for the Tree, and that was the way, the only way, that I could embody the Dance Tree.

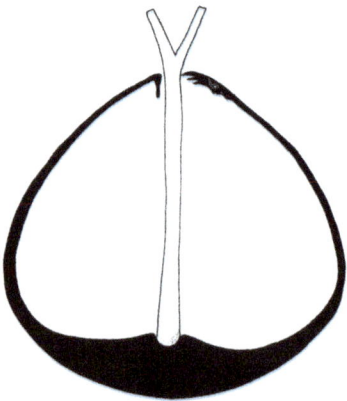

*my body feeds the Tree*

The Grandfather came from behind the Tree. A tree trunk is round, it does not have 'in front' and 'behind', so when the Grandfather steps from behind the Tree he actually steps out of another dimension. I decided to chant his name, and his name came out as: "-ii." Hesitating, I stopped short and he said to me: "What is wrong with a simple name? The simpler: the better." And the name was 'Tree': "Tr-ii" which is time awakening awareness. The Grandfather took me into the Tree, and I stood in the hollowness. I can tell you I felt very different, and it was an extremely exciting feeling to leave my physical awareness and to enter in.

## Tree of Smoke

Friday, I drove down south and stayed until Sunday, stayed, helping my stepmother nurse my father. My father who is drifting away from us, and, I think, going to die. Tomorrow, which is Wednesday, I am going back again to be there and be of help. I was undecided whether to come back or stay, but I think it has been the right thing to come away and consider what is happening, because when I am there I am so deeply drawn into the place where he is that I completely lose my usual way of being. It was good to come away and, when I go back, I will be able to be less swamped by the situation. That is how I inadequately describe what may be maintaining a sense of detachment.

While driving back north on Sunday evening, I saw the most amazing meteor. It was blue-green and left a defined tail as it burned through the atmosphere. It looked just like a large molten ball blazing a clear trail, not at all like the appearance of the Hale-Bopp comet a few years ago which was fuzzy in its outline, devoid of colours, and full of foreboding. This meteor was more like an arcing electrical spark, amazing to see.

I have been with my Father till he died. Dying is such a personal and private event that I did not feel it was appropriate to be recording my experiences of observing the ultimate act of his life. I have come home again for a few days before going back for the funeral.

I came to meditate this morning and I saw the four snakes of the Grandfather; black, and yellow, and green, and blue; they were small but clearly visible in my mind's eye. I looked at them until the picture changed to the australian Sun Moon Dance arbour and I saw Chief Joseph standing there. Joseph carried with him the colours purple and green. Behind Joseph I saw something incomprehensible; a grey shape made of smoke. The lower part was like the column of a nuclear explosion and above it the curls of smoke were like the crown of a great tree. I passed through Joseph and went towards the Tree of smoke. Entering the trunk, I became aware of the Ancient Grandfather and he entered my energy centres, uncompromisingly. Hidden in the smoke of the Tree I laid aside the barriers that I might feel inclined to put up, opened myself, and allowed this to happen.

It was ecstatic and shattering and, after the Grandfather was greater within me than myself, I began to feel the shining essence of the grey horse. The horse was easier for me to understand and easier for me to be and to be able; to be able to be thinking, to be able to be being, and to be seeing and be feeling all at the same time.

I saw that my body was empty, and I came down to land upon a large silver disc that was lying in the emptiness between my navel centre and my heart. I felt that the Grandfather wanted me to look into this shining disc, using it like a mirror to see what was reflected there, but when I tried to do this my own mind, which, of necessity, had to be present, began to panic about producing things that came up to its expectations of what looking in the mirror might entail: visions of the future, for example. I managed to get over this by acting instead of looking. I laid my body face down upon the mirror so that the silver surface was now all of my perception, and I saw a vibrating spot of crystal whiteness, a shimmering oval with grey fibrous trails around the outside edge. A woodlouse was visible to me, legs waving like hair in the wind, and I passed through its silver doorway into another place.

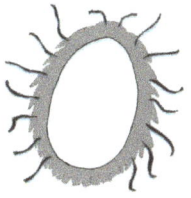

*an ancient doorway*

    This other place was a no-place, a no-time place, a no-form place, and I knew I would see lights. The first light I saw was green. The second light was blue. The third light that came was white, and I became the white light. The white light is inextricably connected to the black, and, as they twisted together, a hole appeared which was the return. The Black Coyote stepped forward to help me and I thanked the Black Coyote for his loving care of my Father's Spirit. The Black Coyote carried me back. Back, maybe, to the sensation of being ........... huh, searching for the right word, ...... involved, encapsulated, um, huh, let's find a good word, .......... into the place of being entered by the Grandfather, en- ........... Let me think again, I need a good word ......... hah, enraptured by the Grandfather!

    I came back. I saw the hollow trunk of a small tree and the Grandfather said to me: "That is the symbol for you. If you see, or feel, or be the hollow tree then you have reached me."

    I came to meditate and very swiftly I saw a flash of the Arizona desert and I saw the profile of the Coyote. I was so pleased to see the Yellow Coyote as he came towards me and touched me with his light; next the Black Coyote approached, and there was a period where I reached out towards the Coyotes and they reached out towards me. Then they became two L-shaped blocks of stone. The Ls were pointing away from each other like bookends; I walked through the gap between them, and, as I passed, I picked them up on my back and carried them both. They were very large, like the stone jambs of a gateway, and we were all laughing because I seemed to buckle over and to practically sink to my knees under this burden. But I made it through and there waiting for me again was the Coyote in a different aspect.

We began to travel. A grey stone came to teach me. I did not expect to hear the stone speak in words, so I took it onto my navel centre in order to enter its energy. The Grandfather came, and we went a long way away from this world. I saw a treaty being signed.

I know that they signed that document not understanding the words which it contained. Specifically, they were lost by the opening words, and what they thought that document was, um, it was not. It was the opening sentences which were the stumbling block. They understood a treaty in a very different way. They understood it to be something like a stone where the agreement came into being in a long process of travelling with the spirits to find out how it was possible to reach an agreement and make a world together which was acceptable to both parties. They saw it as the beginning of a process whereas to the new Americans it was the end of a process. Seeing this brought me closer to this world for a while, and then I travelled again into the atmosphere of the grey stone.

I travelled with the Grandfather, moving with him without the constant construction of reality by my own mind. I asked him a question: "What am I to do?" Nothing was said. We travelled on. Then suddenly I found myself at a place that seemed to be close to my house. I began to sing very loudly and to stamp my feet in a dance that vibrated upon the earth. It surprised me so much that I came right back here very swiftly, feeling that I need to vibrate the energy of the ground at the place where I live and that this is what the Grandfather is asking me to do.

Two weeks have passed since I witnessed the signing of the treaty and it was in yesterday's meditation that I saw a cylinder-shaped red stone object with the top hollowed out and the bottom left flat. Around it, just below the top, there was a slight indentation in the outer surface so that the top section was slightly smaller than the lower one. I had no idea what it was, but I managed to memorize it and bring the image back here.

*the red stone object*

This morning I found that my concentration was very good, and I spent a long time waiting for the right image to come along, letting other things go past. Some of them were interesting and, as they vanished from my memory, I had some regrets that I hadn't held on to them, but eventually, after a long time, the Grandfather came and the whole feeling of the travelling changed.

First of all, I had intense feelings in my body and I began to see colours passing me. Then I saw a Coyote-lined tunnel, black and yellow, half in half. I felt very excited because I knew that we were travelling into another world. The colour blue appeared and then orange, the orange surrounded by and encompassed in the blue. The end result of this journey was that the Grandfather told me that the site of the pipestone quarry is similar spiritually to Uluru. This was not just a question of the colour, although that is very significant, it was to do with the reverence in which the people hold those places. It made sense of the image I saw yesterday which, I now will say, was the bowl of a smoking pipe.

He showed me a musical pipe carved from the pipestone. I have never heard of one of these and I don't know if they exist, but I felt he was saying that, for me, playing the pipe is a similar spiritual practice to smoking the sacred pipe. The sacred pipe has much to do with praying and much to do with peace and much to do with harmony, and, on New Year's Eve, the first of the new millennium, I felt that the musical pipe could be played for world peace. The sound of the pipe would alter perception in a particular way. In playing the pipe for peace, I observed that it was like spirit talking to spirit, it was like the individual having time and giving space.

## Looking for Peace

I came to meditate, and the beautiful spiritual feeling was here. I began to think about the expectations of someone who was talking to me about the coming healing seminar, expectations that the Coyote is going to entertain him during that time. I said to him that the Coyote would not perform on request, like some circus animal.

I called to the Coyotes and they came as rocks. There was a pile of yellow rocks and just one small black pebble from the sea shore. The Black Coyote was the small black pebble, and the Yellow Coyote was in big sandstone lumps. They said to me: "We are rocks; we are moving through time very slowly." The suggestion was that I slowed down too, and I am quite happy to do that. The Black Coyote led me away and down and said to me that he would be working at the healing seminar.

The Ancient Grandfather came, and with him came some new clothes for me, a grey net dress with a round neckline that was decorated with red. The red decoration was composed of small lines at right angles to one another, not in a geometric formation, but staggered so that there was no repetition, an effect achievable by added embroidery rather than in the weave. I remembered seeing this dress before, one night when I was drumming, when I saw a new spirit arriving who was related to the Grandfather. It had made me very joyful then, and now it was coming to me. I wanted to swiftly put it on, but first I needed to do something with my body. I stretched out and explored the physicality of my body, moving my legs and letting them stretch, feeling my creativity lying there. Sensing the wholeness of my pink body, I felt the pleasure of its restricting shape and then it was time for me to wear the dress.

When I entered into the net-ness of the dress, my body disappeared and I became aware of the holes which exist between the threads in the open weave of this garment. I concentrated upon looking through one of the holes. Experiencing the hole-ness, I lay and tried to become nothing that would impede the movement of the Power.

The time came in the seminar to take our journey to the inner temple. I relaxed and, entering the journeying consciousness, I began to travel in the darkness, travelling through a night sky full of silver light. I accepted the darkness, accepted the movement, and began to travel through a series of ancient buildings, one of which had silver light entering through a hole in the ceiling. But nothing happened in these places and I continued to travel on.

I had become resigned to the fact that I would simply travel in the darkness, seeing the occasional temple and sanctuary, till the end of the journey, when I saw ahead of me the head of the Black Buffalo. I said: "I know you! I have seen you before." When I had seen the Black Buffalo, it was struggling to stand, struggling to walk. Now only the head was hanging there in the black space, much larger than myself. I travelled slowly towards it, observing the curly, metallically coloured black coat, the very broad, flat forehead, and the wide spreading horns. In the very centre of the forehead was a golden hole from which issued forth golden light. I put my solar plexus to that golden hole. The image was graphic. The sensation was powerful. Through that hole I went, into the space that is within that Black Buffalo Being.

A surprise awaited me. It was a very peculiar place in there. It was dark, but it was not black, the space was fizzing with whiteness. I felt my awareness of my shape change. I began to lose my body contours and to become, I presumed, the shape of the buffalo, but it was a round contour-less shape that I became, and, after that, absolutely nothing changed. There was a feeling of intense density and pressure, and I only had my awareness left. I had nothing else; the awareness of being fizzing dark matter filled my consciousness. The sensation was not painful; it was not threatening. It was....., I'd like to use the word 'ghastly'. It was a very difficult place to be in because there was nothing to be experienced there except density and pressure.

I searched through my experience for something similar. The only thing it reminded me of was when I was a child, sometimes when I lay in bed at night, my head used to feel very huge. The childhood sensation that went with that was like crunching cotton wool in your hand, but the sensation on this journey was like a pressing weight, an immobile pushing-ness, a kind of suffocation. It did not take my breath; I seemed not to breathe. I distinctly did not like being in there, and, although the sensation was extraordinary and I was certainly questioning what on earth kind of a place it was, I would have very much liked to get out of it, but I couldn't see how that was possible. I seemed to have lost my body, and to have lost the ability to move. I noticed that panic was an option, and I determined to stay calm.

Into the darkness I called very quietly: "Grandfather?" hoping that he would hear and help me. When I called the pressure and the sensation that was so strange began to diminish at once and the strange darkness began to become pure black light. With relief, I knew that the Grandfather would take me out of there, but, as I felt the place diminish, I became aware that somehow this outcome was disappointing. The Grandfather would never make me suffer when I could not stand it, but I felt a sense of defeat in coming out and I chose to go back.

I went back. It was exactly as it had been, and it became very clear to me that I had to surrender in that place because there was nowhere else to go and nothing else to do. I did surrender, and something broke inside me. Something around the level of my solar plexus seemed to be laid upon a block there and broken in half, like a piece of brittle metal. It snapped, and tears rolled out of my eyes. It was a terrible moment because that was the end: that was it.

I don't know what the speckled place was. All I know is that the Grandfather would have taken me out of that state had I persisted in my request, and this proves to me that nothing is done by compulsion in the spirit world. It is all done by choice, and it is very possible that I made the right choice there, to go back, and that pleased the Grandfather. But he would not have been displeased with me if I had come out; I would have been displeased with myself. So that's it: that was my journey to my inner temple. Hah!

I have just travelled with the Grandfather speaking quietly to me about the journey. I hope I never have to travel in through the forehead of the buffalo again, but I suspect it is a metaphor of our world, and maybe an understanding of what it is like to be in this place from the perspective of the bodiless spirit, I don't know. I am just struggling for some insights from this.

The final journey we took during the seminar was to discover our next steps. As soon as the journey started everything went black and I saw the head of the Black Buffalo, which was the Apis Bull, which was the Minotaur, which, as it turned out, was the bull-leapers' Bull from Knossos. The horns of this bull Buffalo Being were golden, gilded, perhaps, for a ceremony; I jumped, leaping through the space between them, using my arms to push me and to give me the impetus to fly.

I travelled upwards into an intense sensation of the Coyote: "Hello, beautiful Coyote, I feel your physical body. I feel your loving presence. I feel the warmth and the heat and the goodness of our connection." We began to travel through space, rolling, rolling together, spiralling and driving onwards through space, travelling towards the boundaries of the planetary atmosphere. This was ecstasy.

I looked down and I saw streams of yellow and black light exiting my feet like spent fuel from a rocket ship. I realized that the Coyotes were burning up and disappearing in the energy of this journey. My euphoria vanished, and I was overcome with grief: I was losing them.

We reached the limits of the atmosphere and they were no longer able to be there. I stood alone at the barrier between this world and something else, seeing a circular hole. The thinnest membrane exists between this world and the next and the hole in it is surrounded by a thin silver rim, which keeps the way open. A voice said to me: "Step through." But I found myself unable to take that step. Instead, I spent a long time minutely examining the silver rim, which is very thin, very fine, and hard and strong as steel. I was grieving over the loss of my power animals. My desolation was intense. I did not want to go on.

I knew I needed to go through the hole, but I could not step, I could not make my feet move, so I led with my head and I tipped off that place and into space. There was no sensation of falling; I drifted, looking but seeing nothing, looking and looking and seeing nothing, feeling rather despairing and still feeling the loss of the beauty and the pictures of the Coyotes and the picture-full world that they live in.

I needed help. I saw Joseph standing in the space there. He was motionless and yet he directed my attention. Looking past him, I saw the form of something like a range of high mountains. I knew that these mountains were the Peace Beings. I tried hard to see them more clearly, hoping to be able to understand what the vision of World Peace is and how it can possibly come about. Try as I might, I couldn't see any more.

One Being stepped forward from the rest of that vast mountain range and that Being gave me a gift of green light. I looked at the green light and I felt myself moving somewhat slightly back towards this place. I was drifting, and I must have drifted near to the hole because the paw of the Coyote came in and he grabbed me. He hooked me, pulled me out through the hole and embraced me fervently. I felt the love come through the thick golden coat of the Coyote and envelop me in a deep and loving embrace. I was so happy that he was still around in order to love me in that way. Within two seconds, it was time to return.

Lying waiting for the group sharing, I began to travel back through the journey. I looked at the silver rimmed hole and I saw that the Peace Being, the one who had stepped forward to give me the light, had come to the portal there and was going to come through. I was shocked. When I was through on the other side I was overwhelmed, feeling that if I could not clearly see the Peace Beings then I would not be able to bring anything back into the world that could help to manifest the vision here, but this Peace Being had come to the portal and was coming through. I called out and I said: "I am sorry. I am sorry to diminish you." As I said this, I hit a whole new wave of grief.

The Peace Being came through the hole and, as it came through, it transformed and became a pink crystal flower. I saw a Rose, a Rose made of rose quartz crystal so that it was strong, long lasting and beautiful. The Peace Being had transformed itself, come here and become that beautiful thing. And there is a Rose, a crystal Rose, which came to me before but was out of my reach.

The Grandfather was with me and he asked me to release all the self-ness that I am holding in my solar plexus. Initially I was reluctant to do this, but I did manage to release all that and to feel the golden circle of awareness which is the solar plexus open. A beautiful feeling, so why is it so hard to release fear? I asked him some specific things: "Grandfather, protect me, Grandfather, help me, Grandfather, guide me." Was that really it? Those words don't seem as powerful spoken in this world. When spoken in the journey there was not just the word 'guide' but all the visual images of the meaning of that word were present at the same time, and so it was an enormous vibration of meaning. Whereas now, when I speak it, it just seems to be a series of rather hollow little sounds. In the meditative world it contained great spaces, great distances, many journeys, and many enveloping feelings of loving protection.

## Crystal Rose

Shortly before I entered the meditative state, the Grandfather was close. I felt him, waiting, ready for me, and immediately I was at the circular hole between this world and the other place. He greeted me as I passed through the hole and sent me in a different direction than the one I went in the seminar journey. He sent me to the left, and he filled my body, starting with my navel centre and slowly moving up through my solar plexus, pausing before entering the heart and allowing me the time to feel his loving presence filling all my awareness. I sensed the Peace Being accompanying the

Grandfather; the Grandfather who is clearly visible in a human form and the Peace Spirit travelling with him who is now visible to me in that place as the pink crystal light.

The Grey Grandfather came very close to me and he had the eyes of a wolf. He stared at me and his eyes came closer and closer to mine until I could only see deep into the eyes of the wolf. I became acutely aware of my navel centre, and I began to see the vast Great Plain, but it seemed empty of animals. Then I spied a brown buffalo there. As I travelled towards it something very strange happened which challenged my prohibitions. I came up behind the buffalo, overwhelming it, and my navel centre closed over it until it was entirely within my body. Was this the wolf hunting down and eating the buffalo? I did not know. Then my navel centre opened wide and buffalo calves, black buffalo calves, were being born in a long line out of my navel centre. Uncurling, they struggled to their feet and shook their bodies, sticky from the birth process and glistening wet, they kicked their legs and they began to run and play. The plain began to fill with buffalo, fill with buffalo, and the Great Plains were going to be no longer empty. They were going to support the life that my Grandfather loved, and that life would return.

I thought: "How crazy it is to be dreaming the dreams of a plains Indian who longs to see that life style re-established." And, while thinking this, also thinking: "How far it is from anything that I have learned to long for from the life I am living now." I saw the meaning of the metaphor; how the spirit plains have become denuded of form and vibrancy, and how this needed to be put right, how, with the Grandfather walking with me, something could be done towards this end.

The Peace Being materialized, and the Rose crystal was visible. Crystal Rose, I called it, and I realized why, of all the flowers, it needed to be a Rose because of the double meaning in that word. The crystal light began to pour through my body and into this place; the rose light was the emanation of Peace. Peace was coming to this particular place here, to my house, as if my house was a channel for the peace vibration to enter the world. The Peace Being said to me: "Always allow." What this meant was always allow myself to be used as a channel in this way and to feel, when I sense the emanations or the spirit Beings coming through me, that I should open up and allow it to be, and I could watch the beauty of this unfolding, and so I did that there and then. I felt the emanations of the pink light pouring through my awareness into this place, and then I felt that the crystal Rose would come to me in a form of this world. I just needed to be aware and wait, and it would come. The emanation faded.

### Returning the White Ribbon

There is a heavy snowfall. I mean that snow is falling now. Yesterday I rang Australia, needing to know when the second Sun Moon Dance is happening there so that I can complete the job that Chief Joseph gave me by carrying the white ribbon back. The Dance was originally scheduled for November, but was delayed, and now I am waiting for the new date. I managed to get the organizers and I was so pleased to hear that the Dance is going ahead in March that I immediately booked all my tickets, so that is that. It is better if I do not think about it because that will only cause me troublesome thoughts in this world. I will just go for it. Joseph has told the new Chief that it is going to be all right, and that is all I need to know.

I returned to Australia carrying the white ribbon to participate in the Sun Moon Dance that was happening over the Easter weekend and I was so glad to be a part of it.

On the day the Dance began, we discovered that there was to be a total ban on outside fires for twenty-four hours in the state of Victoria. There had been a drought since Christmas, many bush fires were burning. The previous night the colour of the setting sun was changed to neon pink by the smoke and gas in the atmosphere. We could not light a fire to heat the sweat lodge stones. What should we do? The lodge was covered, and a gas ring was put in the fire pit and lit. Stones were piled onto this and after three hours the gas ring was removed, and we all piled in for a one-round sweat. The prayers were powerful.

The fire at the entrance of the arbour was laid but not lit, some pieces of red cloth symbolised the flames. I was the only ribbon bearer who had returned to dance, but all the ribbons had been sent back and were present. The Chief asked me to offer them to the fire. I knelt down and took the white ribbon from its bundle. There it was, sacred, just as it had come off the Tree. I picked up the other three ribbons; all had been washed and ironed smooth. I held the four up one by one, showing that they had all returned, and, calling out silently to the Spirit of the Dance Tree, I prayed for the coming Dance. Then I wound them among the sticks of the fire stack, each one at its direction. The next time I came out of the arbour the fire was burning and the ribbons were gone.

## I Am Killed

May day! May day! It is indeed the first of May and this is an emergency. I came home from Australia a month ago, keen to begin work on the Sound Peace Chamber project at my Teacher's place. Phew, well, after several days of extremely challenging events triggered by a video, events which I don't really want to record in detail ............ but I have to give the outlines here.

I had been lent a video on south american medicine men which I took to my Teacher's house. He had looked me straight in the eye and said that he would not watch it without me, but then, as a man under pressure from his partner who well knew what he had promised, did just that. It may not seem much, but when it is my Teacher, upon whose word I utterly rely, it is something rather momentous, to put it in an english way. I got a great shock and, in order to try to find the positive outcome of the incident, I have had to do a lot of very deep work.

The reason for my recording anything is that I meditated this morning and the Grandfather appeared. He was sitting astride his horse on a hill far away, dressed in full regalia. I stayed where I was, noting the distance between us and waiting for him to show me something. He and the horse seemed to lift off from the ground and begin to travel away from me at reasonable speed. It seemed to me that I should not allow the distance between us to increase so I moved myself too, following them and keeping the distance as it was.

As they travelled, they rose up, and soon the Grandfather was surrounded by blue sky. His headdress, which was composed of silver feathers, became a circle, his face vanished and blue sky was visible there. This made a flower in the sky, a blue centre with silver petals, like a daisy. He showed me that when things come to pester me in my meditations, ...... although my meditations are non-existent at the moment, they have become thinking spaces, thinking about the situation and the consequences of what happened, ...... I could take the colour silver and paint over any negative images that were tormenting me, and this would render them incapable of reaching me if I so desired, which is the nitty-gritty of the matter. I feel now that it is possible, through the application of the silver paint, that those negative things could be catalysed, could change, and become something positive.

*the daisy*

There shortly followed three more difficult days. This time hurting my back working too desperately at the chamber site on my own, getting up next day, passing out in the bathroom, hitting the sink, knocking out a tooth........ All the things that went with that; the first disastrous episode triggering the rest.

Last night, when I went to bed, I meditated on the major spirit Beings in my life: the Ancient Grandfather and the Peace Being. The Grandfather came to me and the gathered spirits asked me:

"What do you want?" I said: "I want Love and Peace." After the experience was over, I realized that those words ARE those two Spirits and that I should devote my attention to them.

I came to meditate this morning, having lost some beautiful things that happened to me during the night. I felt immediately connected to my great body travelling space. Where has that been so often during the last few weeks? I don't know. I just felt so grateful to find myself aware in that place again. I tried to memorize the state of mind that brings me there. Then a rush of heat went through me and acute physical discomfort. If I do not withstand this then I cannot travel on, so today I had the desire and the strength to withstand it, and I did.

I began to feel the presence of the loving Grandfather of the Greyness but how different he has become, silver light and the disc of blue, broken into abstractness, such that it is difficult to form any picture. But eventually these shapes did come together and make the image of the Grandfather on his horse wearing the feathered headdress; the feathers silver, the horse silver, the body of the Grandfather a silver grey, his legs, his moccasins, his body, all abstract, made of swift brush strokes with silver paint and just the place where his face would be, blue, a blue disc. Yes, I could accept this: the conventional this-world image of the beautiful Grandfather translated into something more abstract, less attached to the forms of this world.

As I looked at the Grandfather, I felt the Peace Being emanate out of nowhere; right into the centre of my visual field came the pink crystal light that is the Peace Being. As I concentrated one hundred per cent upon this beautiful space, I noticed the body of a young bear curling around the Peace Being and occupying the left.

I greeted the bear, and I said: "Bear, today is an important day, I know that."

I looked intently at the form of the bear lying there like a crescent moon. Suddenly in my hand I felt the iron ore stone that I picked up in the stony desert the first time I was in Australia travelling to Uluru. The bear had a form in the shape of this stone. I smiled and said: "There are no bears in Australia." The surprising image of a marsupial bear came to me. I looked closely; it was a young Black Bear and, indeed, on the front of his belly he had a pocket. It was like a faux fur pocket that somebody had stitched on. This was delightfully amusing to me and I accepted this bear with his mock pocket.

I took myself into the pocket, and through the pocket, through the belly of the bear in to the internal space. The outline of the bear was black, and the inside of the bear was pure red. I had some insight then about how the colour red is so strongly attached to the colour of blood which, in turn, is so strongly attached to the idea of fighting and bleeding and dying that it has in this world some very sticky associations, places to get stuck. I decided to expand my consciousness into all the contours of the bear and not to remain transfixed by the red interior.

I explored the bear and took on all the aspects and the corners of the bear's psyche; admiring his beautiful black claws and travelling right to the tip of his nose where the muzzle becomes a lighter colour; stroking my face along the lines of his teeth and learning to know the power of the bear's jaws, saying to him: "You can chomp my head in a second if you wish to, but I have no fear of that because I am in you and I will not do that to myself."

Now, although linear time must have continued during this experience, it seems to me, when I am trying to recall it, that it all happened in a flash and now it is difficult for me to string the events back in the original order. But I think it was like this: I became the bear, and I began to think about peace, I began to think about the Chamber project which has ground to a halt, and I prayed: "Help me; help me to enter the place where I can, without being blocked by my own psyche, participate in the vision of World Peace and manifest a Sound Peace Chamber." After this prayer I found myself standing beside the bear and when I looked at him, he was purple: "Wow, Bear, you have become purple!" and I knew that Joseph was around.

The Bear and I began to walk towards the horizon. As we walked, I heard: "Fields of wheat." I looked. There was my house, and all around my house were the green fields of wheat, and this was all I needed to keep me on the right path to manifest a Sound Peace Chamber. I considered the word 'wheat': "wh-ii-t", which is breathing awareness moving through time, exactly what I am, and I knew that whenever I became disturbed I simply needed to look at the fields of grain, observe their progress and consider the harvest, and I would remain on the right track, the white track, the way of placement. This was so simple, so already present, and so deeply meaningful to me, that I felt completely satisfied.

## A New Beginning

Last night I worked upon the story I am writing called *Seeking the Vision of World Peace*. I noticed when I came to bed that this had had a profound effect upon me and that it was a good thing to have done.

I came to meditate this morning and I emptied myself, praying to the spirits to come and teach me and help me to be better than I was. After a while I saw the sound '-oh' occupying the centre, O, a great hole through which everything moved.

The Grandfather was in the upper right-hand quarter of the medicine wheel, in the North East, and with him was the colour yellow. As I touched the colour, I knew it was his horse. I could feel my spine becoming the horse. My daily mind clicked in and asked me if I really wanted to do anything so basically idiotic as becoming the horse of the Grandfather? I saw what my state of mind is in my daily life and I didn't want to be trapped in that. I put it to one side, saying: "Don't disturb me now. Don't impose your safety limitations upon me now." And I determined that I would once again follow the feelings of becoming the Grandfather's horse. I saw the letter A. The lower section of the A formed the legs and the back of the horse. The inverted V-shape above was the Grandfather, silver grey, coming to sit astride the yellow horse below.

As the Grandfather rode the horse and came to occupy the totality of my awareness, I saw him stand between myself and other things that are out there. I had the appreciation that the Grandfather is a filter of protection and that through him only helpful things will come. All the other things that might be drifting out there would not come into my dreaming body and cause me concern. I spent some time investigating this filter idea and saw the Grandfather lying over the top of my awareness like the final protective layer of the planetary atmosphere. I asked myself some certain things, like: "Do I really believe in that?" My answer, after careful observation and consideration, was: "Yes, I do." That was a very significant moment because I had my trust in the filter system that all of this was for the benefit of all Beings, and I prayed that I could bring the light, the feelings, the experiences, that I had out there back into the world with me. But now that I am back here, I want to put them into a cupboard and live a 'normal' life, as if I can't see how I can live in the modern world carrying that beauty with me. Hum? ........ help!

## The Blue Light

This morning I have taken the most incomprehensible journey which, to my detriment, I have to say that I fought most of the way. I began to meditate, after a while I found myself in a no-place where the hot sweat began to torment me, and I really determined to get through. For too long recently I have stood at this particular barrier unable to make the effort to go through.

In the darkness, I began to sense an animal. It was a horse. A horse? fff-wur, suddenly my most un-favourite animal, but that was all that was there. I put my hands upon its neck, my body threw itself upon its back, and there I felt the Grandfather, but a most peculiar representation of him, very determined, very strong, very forceful. Something was definitely going to happen, and my querulous little thought was: "Where is the loving Grandfather?"

The Grandfather drew me backwards into himself, into the blue circle surrounded by the silver rays, and for one beautiful moment I was there in the blue, a glorious, timeless moment of perfect placement. Then the Grandfather rolled me up like a ball and threw me backwards so that I somersaulted in the air and came out unrolling. I came to a halt with my belly uppermost. I was in the golden light. My back was grey. My front, which saw, was golden, and the image that I see now is of a woodlouse on its back, unrolled, all fourteen legs waving. Yes, I am sure my consciousness was about as enlightened as that of a woodlouse, and that may be more than I generally exhibit.

Lying there I saw through the blue. The blue light surrounds our world; beyond it we perceive that space is black. That is a perception which members of the human race can now share quite easily. But the Grandfather showed me that beyond the blue light, the light is golden. That is a new direction to travel in, and one into which he has hurled me like a missile.

## Between the Sun and the Moon

I woke this morning, made a cup of tea and felt overwhelmed by the Power while I was drinking it. I lay down and I saw the hoof print of a horse in soft ground. I went to the spirit of the horse and, putting my arms around it, I said: "I do love you, you know."

I was looking at an image of the rainbow, when I saw the shape of the horse's hoof, it was the bow of the rainbow, and a symbolic connection was made there between the power of the horse and the light of the rainbow. It is very possible that I went through the rainbow arch and found there both Joseph and the Ancient Grandfather.

The image that I am left with from that place is ripples of silver running horizontally beneath a blue crescent-shaped boat; above this, like a blanket lying in the boat, a thin concave band of green; and above that, the Sun.

The image built in this way: the central blue disc from the abstract image of the Grandfather, was taken on by Joseph and, in that transition, became the blue crescent which floated upon the silver petals of the original symbol. The petals had become water, which is the carrier of light, and only in the form of water can the light lie and vibrate horizontally. The boat was floating there upon the water when the Sun burst forth and placed its body into the ark. It was at this point that the green line appeared between the disc of the Sun and the crescent of the Moon.

*the transmission of teachings*

## Meditative Dreaming

When I came to meditate this morning, a letter of the alphabet took my attention, it was the letter C. Now, when I had investigated the sounds that the letters made, not in the meditative space, but sitting at my computer, I found that C does not have its own sound. It is either '-k', a K, or '-s', an S, and I thought: "Well, it might as well be left out." Today the letter C appeared in front of me in the meditative space and I thought: "Well, it had better be left in." I have become wise enough to know that things I think with my intellect can be very destructive to spiritual teachings. I stayed with the letter C and eventually I noticed: "It is the shape of a Sound Peace Chamber" and I noticed: "It is the shape of a Sound Peace Chamber under construction."

The Ancient Grandfather came through the open doorway into the centre of the Chamber. A long process followed where I welcomed the Grandfather, observed the Grandfather, and recalled what I know of the Grandfather, Hollow Tree, and wondered how this C-shape of an open oval connected to the Grandfather. Where did this image of the C fit to the image of the Hollow Tree which is the name of the Grandfather? His name is what the Grandfather helps me to become: a hollow tree. Eventually I saw a slice, a cross section of a wooden pipe. If a slice were taken through the exact place where one of the sound holes is that would make the shape of C.

I was almost back to daily consciousness when the mystery of the sound of the letter C returned to me, a letter which has a shape but does not have its own sound, a no-sound letter. That is the teaching about the sound of C, and, of course, there is no sound with seeing.

Days later the next letter, D, was waiting and I saw the D as an eye that was looking back. I became aware of the great art of seeing behind, and none of it was about looking into my own past. For a while I entered into the experiences I have had when I become aware behind myself and find the expanding spiritual feelings which encompass me.

I went to the vertical line of the D and put my hands upon it, it was like a column of vertebrae. I felt the individual vertebra and observed the flexible column snaking upwards. Then D lay down upon the ground and the vertical line became my own spinal column lying against the nurturing body of Mother Earth. Hidden within each vertebra was the silver light of the spinal fluid, and, from in between each pair of vertebrae, the spinal fluid ........ leaked out, might be the right phrase, and began to penetrate the earth with fine roots. I remember them reaching right down to the blue core, receiving nourishment from there.

I saw the line of the meditative body, slightly curved with the curvature of the Earth, lying on the ground with the silver roots entering the body of the Mother to speak to the spirits of the core. My solar plexus was open and, as I looked at the body from a distance, smoke seemed to exit from my solar plexus and form a column in the still air. This was an expression of divine longing, and it felt to me as if this column of smoke could condense and turn itself into a great Oak Tree, but that did not happen today, it was only a possibility.

*meditative dreaming*

Eventually I called: "Grandfather." The Ancient Grandfather responded, and I knew that looking back is the connection to ancientness, a connection which gives me the ability to be rooted and to rise in my awareness eventually forming a great Tree, but initially only able to produce some very formless and insubstantial smoke-like intent, or creativity, or contribution.

Completely absorbed and far away from my own agenda, I lay on my back. The Grandfather was in my mind-awareness, filling my mind with blue light. I really felt that when the time was right, I could enter again the blue light, and, perhaps, that is where I am trying to go now with my own desire and volition and intent. But, although I have this emotional desire, this mental volition, and this spiritual intent, I can't just go there; maybe one day, with help, I will find myself there.

## The Grandfather Dies

Yesterday I woke from a dream in complete disharmony with the world and I could not get the day together at all. That evening, late into the night, I was typing up a tape on my computer (though I wanted to be idle, I had forced myself to do this) when the telephone rang. It was my Teacher saying: "Shall we all plant some willow trees tomorrow?" We went on to discuss what time to meet and I said: "I am picking the others up at twelve, is that too early?" He replied: "No, I am getting up early these days." And I said: "Yes, you are so bloody unpredictable."

This reply had started off inside me as a joke, but when it reached the surface it was like a grenade with the pin pulled and it blew up in my hands. I felt the shock wave hit the target and bounce back at me and I reeled at the incredible disrespect in this remark. Nevertheless, the conversation carried on pretty nicely but when I came off the phone, I began to beat myself up over the hopelessly inappropriate thing that I had said. I felt: "Well, I can either just kill myself right now or I can take this whole situation apart and find out why this popped out of my mouth." Because this is not the first time that this kind of bomb has come out of my mouth and hit another person.

Last night when I went to bed, I looked for help from the spirit world. I was not crying, I was not full of self-pity, I had no feeling that I was a victim, I had no sense of guilt; I acknowledged that the bomb came from me, was mine, was unpleasant, and that there was something that needed to be addressed. I called the name of the Grandfather and immediately the Grandfather was there seated on his horse; they were turned away from me, pointing to the West. I touched the haunches and the Grandfather walked the horse.

I came up beside him to ask him for help, but when I reached him, he had slumped forwards and it seemed to me that he might be dying. He was dying, he told me so. His body fell apart, leaving a pile of bones that slipped off the horse's back, and there, in my arms, was a nest of golden bones.

I knew I had to mount the horse and become a messenger of love. Oh, I really had no ambition to do this. I was begging the Grandfather to return because I knew that he could not die in the way that I feared, but the back of the horse was now bare. I called to my Teacher. Perhaps he did not hear, I do not know, but it was me who had to mount the horse. And I did.

I looked towards the horse's head. There was a demon standing there. I did not want anything to do with this demon. I wanted to say: "Go away" but I knew this response was not right. Help was needed and I needed to give that help. I addressed the demon, asking it to embrace love and I offered one of the golden bones in order to effect this transformation. If the demon would place one of the bones in its body, it would be able to enter the light.

From the effort I made came an understanding that there is an intense transformation happening which I probably cannot rationally understand, but I must keep myself alert because somewhere in my Being I do know how to do this job.

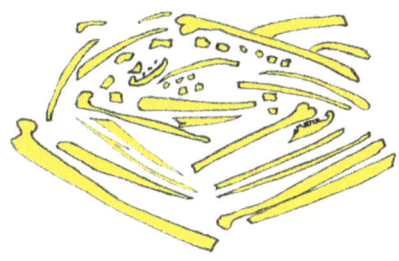

## About Demons

There are no concepts and no descriptive words that exactly apply to many of the experiences to be had in altered state travelling, and while travelling there can be no attempts at explanation because the experience flows, and theorizing freezes it.

As a result, in relation to demons a concept to describe exactly what kind of manifestation they are is missing from my recordings, but clearly, I knew what I was perceiving and chose that word. Now I can think about it.

The demon I encountered was not an entity with independent energy out to corrupt and destroy, it was lost, it was coming out of nowhere. From this I conclude that a demon is a being whose vibration has no connection with other beings; it is a being in isolation. Perhaps, because it has no connections, it cannot even be said to be 'a being'.

Nothing about such demons is visible, but in ceremony and trance travelling, I seem to be able to perceive them and to offer them help. It is not a question of inviting them into my energy field but of giving them the opportunity to engage in movement and make a connection with the light.

Many years after the time of this story, I was dancing in ceremony, dancing from my resting place to the sacred tree and back again. On one return I noticed a demon close by my place. I said: "Come! Come to the Tree with me." The reluctance was palpable, but why else would it be there? It must be attracted to the light. It took many journeys to and from the Tree and many offers of help before that demon took one step and when it reached the Tree it went up in a great burst of light and I am sure it must have felt relieved.

The thing I did not realize until after I held the first edition of this book in my hands is that when the Grandfather's golden bones fell into me, I was a demon; I was lost, isolated, tenuously seeking connections. Look how many golden bones it took to get some light into me! And I am so grateful that the opportunity came.

**About Intent**

The word 'intent' describes the impetus behind a process and implies dynamism. Intent carries an idea from the formless into form, from thought into our reality.

My intent can be solely focused on personal success or it can be more altruistic. I would call the intent that has the wider concern 'spiritual' because in the spirit world all things are in harmony and remain so. The guardian of that spiritual intent is integrity; I read in the dictionary that integrity is 'wholeness'.

So it is that, to fully access integrity, I need to visit the spirit world. My quest there is not to prove anything, only to become a more helpful human being. Occasionally in my altered state work, when I have been having problems with a person in everyday life, I have been given a view of their spiritual being and that has profoundly altered my perception. Maybe, I don't get on with them any better in daily life afterwards, but I understand our connection.

The nature of my intent is tested when a project manifesting in the physical collides with other intents. The challenge is to manifest the intent without creating friction. This is important because all the vibrations that go into its creation will stay in it, resonating, and will be part of the future unfolding of that project. This is the point the Ancient Grandfather makes in this book and I imagine that the enemies of Jesus did not check in with the world of spirit.

If I can connect my physical manifestation with the integrity of my spiritual intention and bring it to fruition without disrupting the harmonious energy of creation, without creating discord among the people; that will be the best I can do.

I found these two lines among my notes. I don't know where they came from. Did I write them?

> The light knows the intentions of the heart.
> Without losing myself, I disappeared.

**About Limits**

With multiple origins, an equal-armed cross set within a circle, named 'the medicine wheel' in this book, is a meditation symbol which can be expanded infinitely. Colours are often assigned to it, one for each section, each direction, of the cross. I work with the assignations given by Joseph Rael: Red in the North, Yellow in the East, White in the South and Black in the West; they appear in this book as the starting flag on p.8.

These four colours are the most commonly used. I wondered how that came to be and I saw that in ancient times, in many cultures, these colours were readily available from red ochre and yellow ochre, from black charcoal and white ash. The red and the yellow from mineral-rich earths; the black and the white from burnt wood and other plants; these were the primary pigments for art in the Stone Age.

Association with these colours is ancestral and, once upon a time, so were understandings about the directions: directions of the rising and the setting sun, of the migrations of birds, humans, and other creatures, the flow of the river, the prevailing winds, the movement of the stars, but not the compass.

Not the magnetic compass and not the geometric compass! Not a North which is unrelated to local needs and conditions, and not a perfectly scribed circle with four equal divisions coloured with acrylic paints, nothing like that! not anything as sparse as that! And yet, that is what I have; a medicine wheel that fixes the four directions and describes the limit of my world.

I use the time that I have gained, and other luxuries which the Ancestors did not have, to invite the gatekeepers of the periphery, the Spirits of the Four Directions, into my world to help me expand the boundaries of my consciousness.

## Other Books by this Author

### Tales of Two Coyotes: adventures with power animals

A great deal of fun and some profound suffering are the order of the day (and the night) in this book of 33 shamanic journeys taken while working with various groups of people in seminars led by my Teacher.

There are ten chapters in the book, each one introduced with a colour sketch.

### On Trees

Leaving my 'safe' house and walking alone in remote places, I battle with my personal problems. It is a battle that occupies the majority of my attention but while I am engaged upon it, natural forces come in to play with my consciousness.

This book contains colour photos of the places and the birds that feature in the text.

### Being of Earth

Loving the Buffalo from before I can remember, I am happy to travel through all times and all spaces in their company. I follow their wanderings until we come to the present moment: a place where the future is Green.

Colour sketches are included in the text as an aid to visualization.

related websites: www.peacechamber.co.uk
www.somethingdoeshappen.co.uk

contact the author: stella@peacechamber.co.uk

## Index

| heading | month | page |
|---|---|---|
| *image* | | *page* |
| the messenger of love | | - |
| the mountains of light | | ii |
| leaving traces | | ii |
| light calendar year | | iii |
| how to read the light calendar | | iv |
| (containing September and March) | | |
| 26 month markers | | v-vi |
| The Falling Bones | May | 1 |
| The Girl | June | 2 |
| *the four objects* | | *3* |
| Interweaving Red and Blue | July | 5 |
| The Wake-up Call | August | 6 |
| *the Dance Tree* | | *7* |
| *the starting flag* | | *8* |
| The Name of the Grandfather | September | 17 |
| Help is the Colour Yellow | October | 19 |
| *light tracks* | | *21* |
| *8 energy centres in a body* | | *22* |
| *the Grandfather in the Tree* | | *24* |
| Gifts from the Southern Hemisphere | November | 26 |
| *Uluru* | | *31* |
| Opening the Gates | December | 31 |
| *Kata Tjuta* | | *32* |
| *passing by* | | *37* |
| Exploring the Grey | January | 38 |
| *footsteps* | | *40* |
| Knowing the Ropes | February | 44 |
| *bow* | | *45* |
| *bow-l* | | *45* |

| heading | month | page |
|---|---|---|
| *image* | | *page* |
| A Modern Jumble | March | 53 |
| The Peace Tree | April | 57 |
| *the Grandfather's colours* | | *61* |
| *the steps of the moon* | | *62* |
| Dancing the Grandfather | July | 63 |
| *a dance dress* | | *64* |
| The Circle of Awareness | August | 65 |
| In Relation To | October | 72 |
| Tree | November | 73 |
| *my body feeds the Tree* | | *74* |
| Tree of Smoke | December | 75 |
| *an ancient doorway* | | *77* |
| *walking* | | *77* |
| *the red stone object* | | *79* |
| *impressions* | | *80* |
| Looking for Peace | January | 80 |
| Crystal Rose | February | 86 |
| *moving through time* | | *88* |
| Returning the White Ribbon | March | 88 |
| *leaving traces* | | *89* |
| I Am Killed | May | 90 |
| *the daisy* | | *91* |
| A New Beginning | June | 94 |
| The Blue Light | September | 96 |
| Between the Sun and the Moon | January | 97 |
| *the transmission of teachings* | | *98* |
| Meditative Dreaming | February | 99 |
| *meditative dreaming* | | *101* |
| The Grandfather Dies | March | 102 |
| *the nest of bones* | | *103* |

www.ingramcontent.com/pod-product-compliance
Lightning Source LLC
Chambersburg PA
CBHW061802070526
44586CB00023B/2671